THE CENTER IS EVERYWHERE

The Center is Everywhere

*Christianity in Dialogue
with Religion and Science*

SEUNG CHUL KIM

☙PICKWICK *Publications* · Eugene, Oregon

THE CENTER IS EVERYWHERE
Christianity in Dialogue with Religion and Science

Copyright © 2022 Seung Chul Kim. All rights reserved. Except for brief quotations in critical publications or reviews, no part of this book may be reproduced in any manner without prior written permission from the publisher. Write: Permissions, Wipf and Stock Publishers, 199 W. 8th Ave., Suite 3, Eugene, OR 97401.

Pickwick Publications
An Imprint of Wipf and Stock Publishers
199 W. 8th Ave., Suite 3
Eugene, OR 97401

www.wipfandstock.com

PAPERBACK ISBN: 978-1-6667-3556-7
HARDCOVER ISBN: 978-1-6667-9276-8
EBOOK ISBN: 978-1-6667-9277-5

Cataloguing-in-Publication data:

Names: Kim, Seung Chul, author.

Title: The center is everywhere : Christianity in dialogue with religion and science / Seung Chul Kim.

Description: Eugene, OR: Pickwick Publications, 2022.| Includes bibliographical references and index.

Identifiers: ISBN 978-1-6667-3556-7 (paperback). | ISBN 978-1-6667-9276-8 (hardcover). | ISBN 978-1-6667-9277-5 (ebook).

Subjects: Religion and science. | Religion—Philosophy. | Religious pluralism. | Christianity and other religions.

Classification: BL240.3 K549 2022 (print). | BL240.3 (ebook).

Contents

Acknowledgments

The author would like to thank the following for permission to draw on previously published material at various points in the composition of this book:

"How Could We Get over the Monotheistic Paradigm for the Interreligious Dialogue?" *Journal of Interreligious Studies* 13 (2013) 20–33.

"An Asian Christian Theology in Dialogue with the Buddhist Philosophy of Keiji Nishitani." In *L'esperienza religiosa tra Oriente e Occidente: Iden-tità in dialogo, a cura di Adriano Fabris*, (Lugano-Siena: Eupress ftl-Edizioni Cantagalli, 2019), 19–30.

"Things Violent in Religion and Politics: Some Critical Remarks on the Theology of Religious Pluralism." *Fu Jen Religious Studies* 42 (2021) 175–91.

In memory of my teachers
Sun Hwan Pyun
and
Heinrich Ott

Preface

Religion and science offer two fundamental ways of understanding ourselves and the world. Each in its own way reaches deep into the core of human existence and its ultimate concerns. To enter into dialogue with religion and science is never a mere intellectual exercise. For the Christian theologian in particular, it invites an existential engagement with what to believe and how to express that belief.

The argument presented here begins from the hermeneutical insight that Christian faith in our times is shaped first and foremost by its dialogue with religion and science, and that it is the task of theology to synthesize faith, religion, and science in terms intelligible to believers today. To demonstrate this, I will look specifically at Christianity's dialogue with Buddhist thought and biological science. The task cannot be undertaken by observing the faith from a neutral standpoint. Like a geologist who sets out to map the strata beneath the surface, the theologian in dialogue must dig deep into the *terra incognita* underfoot in order to understand the events that brought the faith to where it is today.

As a Christian living out my faith within the religious heritage of Asia, I have tried to examine how the Buddhist understanding of reality and the worldview of biological science continue to shape my understanding of the faith. In more general terms, I am convinced that intellectual honesty prohibits us from isolating the self-understanding of the faith from the impact of other faiths and the scientific worldview. I have no illusions that the changes required of the received theological paradigms will sound radical, all the more so because I will suggest a Buddhist approach as an alternative to current approaches to Christianity's dialogue with religion and science. Even so, I am left with the feeling that I have barely gone beneath the surface.

Thomas Merton once wrote that certain places from our past remain special throughout life as gateways to the soul. He himself began the account of his spiritual journey by recalling the smell of his grandmother's room when he was a boy. In my case, two places come to mind from my graduate school days as a naive, young apprentice flush with hope of entering into service to the Queen of the Sciences.

While at the Methodist Theological Seminary in Seoul, Sun Hwan Pyun (1927–1995), a leading representative of interreligious dialogue in Korea, permitted me the use of his office for the duration of my studies in the master's program. I still have a vivid image of that room, lined with books whose margins were full of cryptic notes that set my imagination ablaze.

Later, at the University of Basel, my *Doktorvater* Heinrich Ott (1929–2013) offered me an apartment, rent free, for more than three years. Under the guidance and paternal concern of this eminent theological mind, whose presence I felt every morning as I got up and every evening as I went to sleep, I came to know the adventure and the joy of wrestling with modern philosophical and religious thought.

There are no words to express my gratitude to James Heisig, my senior colleague at the Nanzan Institute for Religion and Culture and professor emeritus of Nanzan University. Retirement has not slowed him down and our daily interactions continue to be a source of advice and encouragement. The time he generously devoted to going over this book with me has made me clarify my thoughts on too many questions great and small to mention.

I would also like to thank Robert Roche, Jr., for his attentive proofreading of the completed manuscript and valuable suggestions. My thanks also go to my colleagues at the Nanzan Institute, especially to Tim Graf, who helped me find the right way to render difficult German passages into English.

Even after these many years, I am indebted to Yokote Masahiko and his wife Takako, who arranged an academic position for me in Japan, and to Endō Keiko who supported me as I settled into life in Japan. Throughout it all, my parents, my wife In Hwa, and our two children, Se Yung and Hee Yung, have kept me anchored in the things that matter most and kept me from getting lost in the world of ideas. Many ideas and turns of phrase in this little book occurred to me on evening walks with my wife, who time and again stood by patiently as I stopped to jot down a note to myself.

If there be anything of value in what follows, it is a credit not only to those whom I have mentioned by name but to all those others whom space prevents me from listing. My hope is that the errors and oversights that remain through no fault of theirs in no way dim the light of their contribution.

Seung Chul Kim
Nagoya, Japan
20 May 2021

"Deus est sphaera infinita cuius centrum est ubique, circumferentia nusquam"

— *Liber XXIV philosophorum, 2*

1

Religion and Science as *loci theologici*

In any attempt to define itself today, Christian theology is bound to find itself entangled in controversy with religion and science. Whatever its starting point and whatever its method, it has no choice but to engage the questions that the critical study of religions and the scientific explanation of religions pose to it. No doubt, these are among the most urgent *loci theologici* of our times. As such, they need to be faced head-on and without fear of the consequences. In each age, theology has to come to terms with its particular historical conditions, its *topos*. Today that *topos* is framed by religion and science, which has called into question the very conditions for the possibility of doing theology. As the varieties of its response over the past decades attest, one thing has become clear: religion and science represent a legitimate and necessary place for theology to reflect on its methods and carry on its task of guiding faith to understanding.

THEOLOGY AS A HERMENEUTICAL PROJECT

As an academic discipline, Christian theology is always an interpretation of faith in the world in which it finds itself. Its identity and self-understanding are rooted in this hermeneutic task. Without straying off into the complex history of theology's relationship to hermeneutics, let us pause for a moment at the term *self-understanding*. What German philosophy calls *Sich-verstehen* or *Selbstverständnis* is more than a psychological or epistemological concern. Understanding oneself "always occurs through understanding something other than the self, and includes the unity and integrity of the other."[1] It is never a solipsistic self-consciousness but an integrated reality that opens a human being to what lies beyond the solitary self. So, too, *understanding* is much more than the accumulation of facts, information, knowledge, and technique that we rely on to control our surroundings and bestow familiarity on the unfamiliar. It is an event of experience that discloses the meaning of the world and our distinct mode of being human within it.[2] When we understand something, in the authentic sense of the term, this shell I call "myself" is cracked open to something "other." The act of understanding is "the movement of transcendence, of moving beyond the existent."[3] When we understand, we experience ourselves and the world anew. We project (*entwerfen*) ourselves out of our present selves and into our possibilities. This is what Hans-Georg Gadamer means when he states that "all such understanding is ultimately self-understanding."[4] We exist in virtue of the self-understanding that makes us who and what we are.

As for the hermeneutical nature of theology, Heinrich Ott draws our attention to a passage from the New Testament: "Always be ready to make your defense to anyone who demands from you an accounting for the hope that is in you" (1 Peter 3:15).[5] Insofar as the fundamental task of theology is to give a reasonable account in response to questions put to it, that task belongs to a broader responsibility to its own innate historicity. Ott continues:

> The idea of giving an account... deepens our understanding of the inherent historicity of theology. We do not have to account for *every* question posed at each moment of every age. If questions have their own historicity, so does the accountability of theology. There are times in history when specific questions become *topical* (*aktuell*), and specific answers become possible that had not been available before.... Therefore, as human beings confined by history and the finitude of life, theologians can only be responsible and accountable for what happens within their history. Their thinking is bound by the questions and answers that are possible at their own time, meaning that they will never achieve a timeless truth system. Despite this incompleteness and historical conditioning, theological thought remains committed to truth and knowledge of the truth. Without forsaking its historical limits, it rises nonetheless to a corresponding truth.[6]

There we have the heart of the theological endeavor. By limiting theologians to "the questions and answers that are possible at their own time," Ott does not mean to question the ability of individuals engaged in theology. His point is rather that, because all theological themes belong to history, no theologian at any given time can ever embrace the totality of questions that have been handed down in tradition. Indeed, the limitations of history prevent theologians from arbitrarily deciding which themes to take up and which to ignore. This is not to say that they have no choice in the questions they deal with, only that their choice should not ignore the conditions under which they carry out their task. The range of questions put to theology at any particular time are a historical given. As such, they mirror the dual responsibility of theologians to their discipline and to their age. Any particular *topic* a theologian takes up for consideration necessarily reflects the place or *topos* within which their thinking is done.

That so many have fixed on questions raised by the encounter between religion and science as the most urgent task of theology is hardly to be wondered at. But precisely because they are "topical" (*aktuell*), they demand "specific" answers that are "possible" now even if they "had not been available before." There is more to Ott's term *aktuell* than words like "current," "prevailing," "relevant," or "contemporary" can convey. It suggests a *topos* where the "topic" takes shape and where theology is held to account in response to it. We shall have more to say of this in the next section.

The insight into the historicity of theology as both restricting and enabling the specific questions and answers that theologians have at their disposal may be extended to individual believers who understand themselves as historical beings and understand the truth of their faith as something that has been revealed historically. The insight into historicity enables one to be part of the ongoing event (*Ereignis*) of the faith tradition. Put the other way around, the tradition of faith is best understood as an event in the making when one has first accepted oneself as a being limited and enabled by specific historical conditions. Faith is neither the autonomous working of the believer nor a heteronymous imposition from without. It is an event in which the hidden reality of self and world are brought to light. To be authentic, faith requires understanding. The two belong together, and in this sense, faith is no less hermeneutical in nature than understanding is. The tradition of faith transmitted through history is, of course, the indispensable foundation for genuine belief. Only when that tradition, as past, becomes the foundation of our being here and now in the present can it become an historical expression of our most authentic self. Only then can we say that we *understand* the tradition and that the tradition has been *transmitted* to us.

Set against a broader perspective, the idea of historicity of theology as a self-understanding of Christian faith is rooted in the historicity of understanding itself. As Gadamer has argued so memorably, all understanding is bound to a historical standpoint. Understanding "takes place," which accounts at once for its limitation and its potential. At the same time, it is never bound to any one place or set against any one "horizon." As human consciousness shifts through time, so do horizons move and fuse. At the same time, because a particular horizon is presupposed in every act of understanding, there is no way to explore a horizon thoroughly. It retreats at every step we take towards it. Even to inquire into the horizon assumes the presence of an unconscious horizon, and so on in infinite regress.

The historicity of understanding means that we are "always already affected by history." We are already under the influence of the tradition whose meaning we seek to understand. The tradition is not a neutral object there for our understanding; there is no way to take historical distance from it. "Historically effected consciousness is an element in the act of understanding itself and... is already effectual in finding the right questions to ask."[7] Thus, for example, understanding a text occurs under the influence of the history that sets the text before us, and that history "determines in advance both what seems to us worth inquiring about and what will appear as an object of investigation."[8] In this sense, the tradition we seek to understand cannot be seen as separate from our search, like some object standing on its own. It is more like a person that calls out to us and touches us. As Ott puts it:

> The situation specific to hermeneutical realization—namely, that the object of realization is itself the subject who does the realizing, and that the very act of realization so changes the relationship between the two (basically disintegrating the traditional notion of a subject) that it can never produce definitive, fixed results (thus making "verification" impossible)—is probably best expressed by the idea of *dialogue.*[9]

In other words, understanding represents a kind of ongoing dialogue with the text, a question-and-answer exchange between the reader and the read. I am reminded here of an image the Romanian-born German poet Paul Celan used in a speech delivered on the occasion of being awarded the prize for literature from Free City of Bremen in 1958, where he likened a poem to a message in the bottle:

> Since it belongs to language and is therefore essentially dialogical, a poem can be a message in a bottle thrown out to sea in the confidence—certainly not always the hope—that it may someday wash up on land somewhere, perhaps on the shore of the heart. In the same way, poems are under way: they are heading toward something. Toward what? Toward some open place that can be inhabited, toward a thou which can be addressed, perhaps toward a reality which can be addressed. Such are the realities at stake in a poem.[10]

Say you find a bottle that a wave has washed ashore. Inside there is some kind of message. You take it out and open it, only to discover that it is written in an unknown language with a cryptic script. You suspect it to be a secret mythical text of some sort. You cannot say quite why, but the piece of paper fascinates you and your first thought is to have it translated in order to know what it says. Who sent it, from where, and to whom are all a mystery, but something in you wants to send a reply. Strangely, you believe that you will understand the message once it has been decoded, and perhaps that it will tell you something new about yourself. The more you think about it, the more the hope grows in you that even if you never understand it completely, nevertheless you will learn something about its origins and purpose. The text has become a kind of "open place that can be inhabited," directed towards a personal "thou which can be addressed." Yet try as you might, it remains an unfathomable other. As Gadamer remarked of Paul Celan's collection of poems *Atemkristall*: "The thou is an 'I' as much and as little as the I is a self."[11]

If we follow Gadamer in seeing understanding as an ongoing "fusion of horizons" that can be compared to a dialogue between living persons, its essence is best captured by a logic of question-and-answer. Hence, to understand a text stemming from a particular set of historical conditions, we have first to understand it as an attempt to answer a specific question. But to identify the question, we have to recast it in terms that make sense to us, and that means detaching it from its original horizon and setting it in our own. For all questions are "asked in particular historical circumstances," and understanding these questions means "understanding the particular presuppositions whose demise makes such questions 'dead.'"[12] Throughout it all, our pursuit of the question is aimed at understanding history.

The same insights into the hermeneutic nature of theology that Ott came to from the perspective of a systematic theologian expressed may also be found in Bernhard Lohse, a historian of Christian doctrine, who concluded that dogmas and creeds, as specific interpretations of specific theological topics, "age" through time:

> The continuity of the church and its history of dogma does not change the fact that dogmas and creeds from the past can become obsolete. The aging of particular determinations and teachings is unavoidable. We see this process at work time and again. Even in our present day, one can see how some creeds formulated only yesterday to cover the whole of human existence no longer appeal to people, because things have completely changed for them in the meantime.... The fact that creeds age indicates a continuing shift of emphasis in the way dogma is questioned and the challenges posed to it. It is not only a matter of supplementing old truths but of presenting the whole truth in every newer form..[13]

By admitting that creeds age, Lohse does not intend to do away with the "continuity of the church" but to preserve it and to underscore its pursuit of an ever clearer understanding of the unfolding truth of dogma. In other words, the situation or *locus* from which questions of dogma are taken up is never permanent or stable, and yet the whole truth is revealed at every moment and through every change of historical circumstances. For Lohse, Christian theology has always sought the essence of the faith by putting questions to it different from those of other times. In the fourth century, attention was fixed on the doctrine of the Trinity and the divine identity of Father and Son. In the sixteenth century, theological arguments tended to concentrate on ways of salvation. Given this historical nature of theological understanding, we are obliged to raise suspicions regarding the presuppositions under which theologians are working today.

> It may well be that in our own day, actual decisions about what is Christian and what is non-Christian are to be made in a *place* (*Stelle*) altogether different from what many expect, and that later generations will be at a total loss as to how the majority of people failed to see the actual questions at stake.[14]

Drawing on examples from the history of creeds and dogmas, Lohse lays out how each age has had its own particular slant on topics it had singled out for attention. Each stage in the history of Christian thought is *topical* in the twofold meaning described above: it works from a distinctive hermeneutical "place" and works on certain issues identified as relevant. The place (*Stelle*) from which theology is done is as provisional as the historical situation that defines it. Simply put, if understanding is irretrievably historical, then there is no path for a contemporary thinker to recover the past conditions under which a specific dogma was first formulated and present an unblemished account of the meaning it had in its pristine state. To recall Gadamer's insistence, the questions we compose to approach a text can never be set against the same horizon as the original text.

Among the many factors that frame the hermeneutical situation of contemporary theology, religion and science stand out as crucial. But a theology that is hermeneutically alert to the variety of disciplines that comprise our contemporary idea of "religion" and to the full philosophical and technological consequences of "science" as we think of it today, is a theology that finds itself in serious trouble. The deeper its dialogue with religion and science, the more violent the shaking of its foundation. The questions being posed by religion and science are more than a passing challenge that contemporary theologians can weather by clarifying their methodology, recommitting themselves to the faith, and biding their time. Aside from the intellectual demand of dealing with those questions seriously, received images of what it means to be a Christian and to see the world through Christian lenses no longer seem as reliable as they once did. The seamless robe of belief has grown threadbare and insecure. As we shall see later on in this chapter, theology has had to step down from its pedestal of ages past and admit that Christianity is only one among many religions in the world. The conviction that it held in its own hands the exclusive means for salvation, and that the truths of its creed were absolute for all times and places, is no longer sustainable. Yet even as theology struggled to adjust to the reality of religious pluralism and the threat of doctrinal relativism, it has still to contend with the mounting pressure from the natural sciences—particularly from post-Darwinian biology—to discard religion as a vestigial by-product of human evolution. The very fidelity to its vocation that urges theology to take the data and methods of science seriously seems to be asking it to betray its own tradition. But what tradition are we talking about here? And what form of betrayal?

Lohse, we recall, argued that the "place" to interpret Christian dogma as a crystallization of the faith is specific to each generation, such that the questions "at stake" in one age often prove unintelligible to the next. For us today, that place is defined by the encounter with religion and science. These are the *loci theologici* on which the identity of Christianity hangs in our time, so much so that to the extent that the self-understanding of Christianity is *not* shaken to its roots, we may say our theology is radically displaced. The places in which theological reflection sought refuge in the past have either collapsed or vanished from view.

Theology would seem to find itself in the crossfire between religion and science, each of which targets Christianity's claims to absolute truth in its own way. Might it not it be possible for theology to step into that crossfire willingly, not as an act of renunciation but as an act of courage, standing up to that "two-edged sword, piercing until it divides soul from spirit, joints from marrow (Hebrews 4:12)? Might not the critical questions being thrown up by religion and science reach deeper than their often adversarial surface, driving Christian theology to a new place from which to fulfill its hermeneutical task of "answering everyone who asks you to give the reason for the hope that you have"?

For my part, I am persuaded that advances in the study of religion and science can help theology shed new light on much that it had obscured or forgotten in its effort to defend itself against the onslaughts of the age. The questions religion and science pose to theology can be an occasion for the "revelation" of hitherto neglected aspects of Christian self-understanding. Such a revelation is not only possible, it is necessary. The range and intensity of the theological response to the challenge of religion and science over the past decades also are evidence of how deeply Christianity has been cut to the quick. At one extreme we see a ferocious defense of the tradition; at the other, polite gestures of appeasement. Elsewhere along the spectrum we see the birth of theologies of religion, theologies of interreligious dialogue, theologies of religious pluralism, and theologies of science. The consequences for Christianity's future as theology ponders its *salto mortale* into the dialogue with religion and science could not be more momentous.

THEOLOGY AND RHETORIC

Earlier I hinted at my reasons for translating Ott's term *aktuell* as "topical." I return to the point now in order to shed further light on the hermeneutical nature of theology and to clarify Lohse's reasons for stressing the place (*Stelle*) for identifying the questions at stake in our interpretation of dogma.

As is well known, the word *topic* has close ties to rhetoric. It stems from the Greek τόπος, meaning "place." *Topica*, Aristotle's classic treatise on rhetoric, was a series of reflections on the meaning and function of *topos*. "Rhetoric" is often associated with the skillful wordplay of the sophists, due in part to Plato's hostility against it. In the *Gorgias*, Plato describes it as a technique for persuading ignorant people through flattery, not unlike unhealthy food made to look savory or an uncomely visage camouflaged by cosmetics.

For Aristotle, in contrast, the aim of rhetoric is "to discover a method by which we shall be able to reason from generally accepted opinions (ἔνδοξα) about any problem set before us and shall ourselves, when sustaining an argument, avoid saying anything self-contradictory."[15] Rhetoric differs from argumentation based on accepted principles that we see in the objective proofs of the natural sciences. It is hermeneutical in nature and its aim is persuasion. It does not exclude emotional agreement or personal judgment. Its idea of truth is not self-evident but probable, not objective and neutral but subjective and practical.[16]

Cicero, who adapted Aristotle's *Topica* for the Latin world, defined the goal of rhetoric as a theory of "how one might discover arguments methodically and without fear of error."[17] Rhetoric provides the orator with a *topos* for maintaining consistency in dealing with the *topic* at hand. To this end, Cicero translated the Greek word τόποι with Latin terms for "places": *sedes* and *loci*.[18] For a speech to succeed—that is, for an orator to persuade an audience—the topic must be something both sides share an interest in. *Topos* is like a medicine cabinet. To prepare the right drug for a patient, the pharmacist needs to know not only what ingredients to use but also precisely where they are on the shelf. In this sense, as Aristotle says, *topos* involves the art of memory:

> For just as in a person with a trained memory, a memory of things themselves

is immediately caused by the mere mention of their *loci*, so these habits too will make a man readier in reasoning, because he has his premises classified before his mind's eye, each under its number.[19]

Since the goal of the orator is persuasion, the hermeneutic role of rhetoric does not stop with the choice of a suitable theme. There has also to be a give and take with listeners, which implies dialogue and disagreement. The topic is not presented as a set of facts based on objective principles of logic that preclude different interpretations. It is a hermeneutical hypothesis that requires the input of both the speaker and the audience. Michael Leff notes the ambiguity and sense of adventure that distinguishes this process from argument by ordinary propositional logic:

> Rhetorical arguments generally deal with confused notions, with ideas and concepts that do not admit of a single, unequivocal meaning. Consequently, rhetorical argumentation normally does not begin with fixed axioms in the manner of demonstrative reasoning. Instead rhetoricians must draw their starting points from accepted beliefs and values relative to the audience and the subject of discourse. When these beliefs and values are considered at a high level of generality, they become "commonplaces" or "common topics" for argumentation: the attempt to render a systematic account of such topics therefore has been a major concern of rhetorical theory from antiquity to the present.... The rhetor is a hunter, the argument his quarry, and the topic is a locale in which the argument may be found.[20]

Leff's metaphor of the hunter coincides with our earlier comparison to a pharmacist who needs to locate the proper ingredients to prepare a remedy. Just as the contents of the medicine cabinet are of no use without a prescription tailored to the patient, so, too, it is not enough for one to be well versed in a particular topic under discussion unless one is also alert to the *topos* of one's listeners. If the topic or its presentation is ill fitting, the argument will fail to persuade.

I am reminded here of a remark from Cicero's *De oratore*:

> I have sketched these topics as shortly as a brief possible. For if I wished to reveal to somebody gold that was hidden here and there in the earth, it should be enough for me to point out to him some marks and indications of its positions, with which knowledge he could do his own digging, and find what he wanted, with very little trouble and no chance of mistake: so I know these indi-

cations of proofs, which reveal to me their whereabouts when I am looking for them; all the rest is dug out by dint of careful consideration.[21]

The *topos* is the hiding place of the argument. It has to be searched for like a treasure buried in a field that is worth everything to the seeker (Mark 13:44). The key role that rhetoric played in juridical judgment and political oration faded with the end of the Greek polis and the Roman republic, only to be absorbed into the field of literature.

Around the middle of the twentieth century, the eminent German philologist and critic of romance literature Ernst Robert Curtius resurrected interest across the human sciences in the "rhetorical topic." His pivotal study, *European Literature and The Latin Middle Ages*, was an attempt to uncover a unity of meaning in European literary history by singling out a succession of recurring "topics."[22] To this end, he concentrated his analysis on the poetic tradition from ancient Rome to the Latin Middle Age, which he held to contain the quintessence of all Western literary genres in condensed form. His guiding idea of the topic is contained in the following passage;

> In the antique system of rhetoric topics is the stockroom. There one found ideas of the most general sort—such as could be employed in every kind of oratory and writing. Every writer, for example, must try to put the reader in a favorable frame of mind. To this end, until the literary revolution of the eighteenth century, a modest first appearance was recommended. The author had next to lead the reader to the subject. Hence for the introduction (*exordium*) there was a special topic; and likewise for the conclusion. Formulas of modesty, introductory formulas, concluding formulas, then, are required everywhere. Other topoi can be used only for some particular species of oratory—for the judicial oration or the epideictic oration.[23]

Curtius borrowed his notion of "topic" from classical rhetoric. He considered topics vessels for storing patterns of thought, motifs, images, idioms, plots, and the like from one generation to the next and making them accessible for centuries. In this sense, topics offered an ideal "starting-point and heuristic principle"[24] for exploring the unity of meaning throughout European literature. The topic incorporates such "a bewildering diversity of meanings"[25] that even something as simple as proper etiquette can be seen to hold strata of ethical, philosophical, and theological connotations that have accrued over time. In comparing the topic to a "stockroom," Curtius suggests that the miscellanea of items that make up a given topic form a conglomeration all their own. For example, he refers to topics of "consolatory oratory," "affected modesty," "exordium," "conclusion," "invocation of nature," "the world upside down," "boy and old man," and "old woman and girl." When poets make use of such topics in their poetic compositions, they are participating in Europe's literary tradition. For example, Dante's *Divina Commedia* employs the metaphor of the journey, a literary *topos* since the time of Homer:

> In the *Purgatorio,* Virgil and Dante are joined by the late Roman poet Statius. Dante's last guide and patron in his journey through the other world is Bernard of Clairvaux. Bernard's prayer to the Virgin Mary brings Dante the vision of God which is the final note of the *Paradiso*. For his introductory chord, however, Dante needed his meeting with the antique poets and his reception into their circle. They must legitimize his poetical mission.... Without Homer, there would have been no *Aeneid;* without Odysseus' descent into Hades, no Virgilian journey through the other world; without the latter, no *Divina Commedia*.[26]

However, as Curtius is careful to note, the *topos* works autonomously and unconsciously, like a Jungian archetype, "a literary remembrance flowing into the author's quill."[27] It is not so much that the author uses a *topos* as that the *topos* uses the author. Because it works behind the scene, the *topos* prevents a writer from choosing and elaborating a literary topic arbitrarily. Like the *topoi* of rhetoric, the literary *topos* guides poets towards themes suited to the ideas they wish to express. Echoing Cicero's description of the *topoi* as a hidden treasure, Curtius asserts that "things human and divine lie hidden" in literary topics.[28]

Gadamer's philosophical hermeneutic, his critical inquiry on the phenomenon of understanding, begins with a rehabilitation of the tradition of rhetoric. In so doing, he pits himself squarely against the Cartesian insistence on a universal, objective method for attaining knowledge and guaranteeing its truth. The ancient appeal to rhetoric as an independent path to understanding changed dramatically with the emergence of scientific methods based on material, verifiable evidence. Descartes, Kant, and Hegel, each in his own way, considered rhetoric a restatement of something already known, not as a means to new knowledge. Rhetoric was demoted to a tool for speakers who enjoy "chat."[29] Gadamer, in contrast, considered Giambattista Vico (1668–1744) the forefather of philosophical hermeneutics because he sought the experience of truth not in its objectivity and universal applicability, but in the historicity and probability that characterize the aesthetic experience of art. Vico resisted the Cartesian project of subduing all academic disciplines to the scientific method, arguing that "all disciplines of science must take their beginning from that of the matters they treat."[30] This was Gadamer's guiding precept as well.

The methods of the human sciences do not coincide with those of the natural sciences. Gadamer drew the distinction by turning to Vico's notion of probability (*sensus communis*) as the defining trait of truth in the human sciences. Like the rhetorical concept of probable truth and Aristotle's understanding of *phronesis*, the practical knowledge of what Gadamer calls "intellectual virtue"[31] is charged with liberating hermeneutics from the scientific pursuit of objective precision. Even though the term *sensus communis* refers generally to social virtues of right thinking and right behavior, for Gadamer it implies "a moral, even a metaphysical basis."[32]

When Heidegger described attunement (*Stimmung*) in *Being and Time* as a "fundamental *existentiale*" of the human mode of being, he referred to Aristotle's *Rhetoric* as crucial for the exploration of affect (πάθη), characterizing it as "the first systematic hermeneutic of the everydayness of Being with one another."[33] For orators to succeed in communicating, they must be sensitive to the feelings of their audience. For Heidegger, the same applies to all human interaction. The Being-there (*Dasein*) of human beings which is manifest in the ability to speak and listen turns on the same axis as Aristotle's rhetoric. When the rhetorical tradition was downgraded to an academic discipline in late Hellenism and the Early Middle Ages, something of great value was lost. We need to restore rhetoric to the stature of "the discipline in which *Dasein* understands itself explicitly," that is, to its role in the "hermeneutics of *Dasein*."[34] In short, rhetoric delivers to understanding what is most fundamentally human about us.

The attention Gadamer gave to Philip Melanchthon (1497–1569), the first Protestant theologian and collaborator with Martin Luther, is significant for its emphasis on the importance of philosophical hermeneutics for theology. In *Common Topics of Theology or Fundamental Doctrinal Themes*

(*Loci communes rerum thelologicarum seu hypotyposes theologicae*), first published in 1521, Melanchthon applied the ancient theory of rhetoric to his interpretation of the Christian scriptures. The result, says Gadamer, was nothing short of "epoch-making."[35]

Written in the turbulent climate of a time when the meaning of the Christian tradition was in serious crisis, the *Loci comunes* spanned the disconnect from the old and the transition to the new. In it, Melanchthon helped the Reformation embrace the Renaissance by readjusting the relationships among scripture, tradition, and human reason. In particular, he attempted to synthesize Luther's principle of *sola scriptura* with the Catholic understanding of tradition, ancient Greek rhetoric, and the humanism of Erasmus. Because of his insistence that the teachings of scripture and tradition were not to be repeated but reinterpreted, Gadamer dubbed Melanchthon the forefather of philosophical hermeneutics.[36]

Melanchthon classified the whole of Luther's theology in terms of sin, grace, Law, and Gospel, which constituted "the central topics of the Christian faith, the central themes of Scripture, and the central focus and experience of the Christian life."[37] The *Loci communes* tried to distance Luther's principle of *sacra scriptura sui ipsius interpres*—scripture interprets itself—from traditional theories of biblical inspiration, and to underscore his critique of the Catholic Church's insistence on the indispensability of dogmatic tradition.

In short, the *Locus theologicus* represents a "theological place," a place for doing theology, from which faith can wrestle with topics like God, human existence, Christ, the Holy Spirit, the Church, history, and so forth. Melanchthon was the first Protestant theologian to seek out the right places (*loci praecipui*) in scripture for justifying particular dogmatic claims.[38] Not surprisingly, his *Loci communes* prompted a response from the Catholic side. In a work published posthumously under the title *De locis theologicis,* the Spanish Dominican Melchior Cano (1509–1560) argued that "the church is the place and principle of the faith."[39] Although his conclusions differed, Cano shared Melanchthon's interest in classical rhetoric, which he described as "the dwelling place for all the theological argumentation" (*domicilia omnium argumentorum theologicorum*).

Gadamer's analysis of Melanchthon has given the notion of *loci theologici* a new meaning for our times as well. Note how the following passage from a contemporary theologian coincides with the classical usage of that term in Melanchthon;

> *Loci theologici* generally refer to clusters of organizing principles that help determine the focus of theology. Various biblical themes like sin, redemption, justification, grace, and so forth provide systematic theology with some of its *loci theologici*. The term can also refer to the sources on which theologians draw for their reflections. In this sense, scripture, liturgy, the experience of the faithful, local churches, and the like become important *loci theologici*.[40]

Insofar as "*loci theologici* can also refer to the sources on which theologians draw for their reflection," we may expect the same hermeneutical and rhetorical insights to be relevant to Christian theology today, particularly for locating its encounters with religion and science. Like all attempts of the Christian faith at self-understanding, theology begins as a discourse about the *locus* of its thinking.

To summarize, the *topos* identifies the situation in which a discussion "takes place." It tells us *where* to look for "the right way to take things," *whence* an argument proceeds, and *whither* its persuasive power is headed.[41] The topic is not only a standpoint for posing questions but also for evaluating answers to those questions in dialogue with others. Religion and science have not become topics for theological consideration by choice. They are a given for us, the *topos* in which theology must work. When theologians "initiate" a dialogue with religion and science, they are in fact stepping into a discourse that already has taken root in modern consciousness. The questions have not emerged from their own discipline but have been pressed on them from without.

The woods into which theology ventures to pursue its dialogue with religion and science are dark and unknown. Whatever maps tradition may have left behind from explorations of other forests at other times soon prove unreliable. To navigate this *terra incognita*, the adventurer must become the adventure; the thinker must become the *topos*. It is not the theologian's job to redesign the forest, but to walk it, to listen to its voices and think about how to reply.

OVERLAPPING DIALOGUES

There are any number of remarkable studies on the relationship between religion and science we could single out to shed light on the history and development of these two very different ways of looking at reality. For our purposes here, the most important part of the picture is the overall absence of theology. In part, this is due to its failure to appreciate its methodological distance from a world that has thrown religion and science together. They are not a relevant topic because theology has yet to embrace them on their own *topos*.

By and large, theological advances in the dialogue with religion and science have regarded the two as different and largely unrelated questions. It is as if they stood on opposite sides of the wall, each with its own language and culture, and theology could only deal with one of them at a time. With a few exceptions, which we will come to in the following section, when Christianity has held discussions with scholars of religion or even believers from other faith, it has done so without a second thought for the scientific worldview into which they have all been baptized.

Similarly, in its dialogue with science, the reality of a religiously plural world in the background has been treated as if it were neither here nor there. The fact is, the dialogue of organized religion with science has been monopolized by theologians or specialists in Christianity. Shelves of otherwise excellent treatises on "religion and science" display the same naive conceit: the belief that Christian themes like a personal God, creation, revelation, providence, and the like are a fair representation of the whole of religion.

Let us consider two examples. In his book *Religion and Science*, Ian Barbour reviews the history of the Christian encounter with natural sciences like physics, astronomy, biology, and geology. His purpose is set out in the form of a series of questions:

> What is the place of religion in an age of science? How can one believe in God today? What view of God is consistent with the scientific understanding of the world? In what ways should our ideas about human nature be affected by the findings of contemporary science? How can the research for meaning and purpose in life be fulfilled in the kind of world disclosed by science?[42]

Note how his opening question on "the place of religion in an age of science" slides effortlessly into the question about the possibility of believing God today. Without having to belittle the vast religious heritage of humanity, Barbour would already have had his hands full if he had limited the scope of his question to "the place of Christianity in an age of science."

As it turns out, his examples of the response of religion to science fall all but exclusively within the domain of Christian theology. The controversy between science and the Church over astronomy, the conflict between reason and faith in the debate over Deism, and the bitter dispute over the dangers of evolutionary theory to belief in a creator God are cases in point. Barbour classifies the history of religious responses to natural science in four modes: conflict, independence, dialogue, and integration. But this only extends as far as the Christian faith. Regarding the response of other religious traditions, we are told very little. I found only a handful of allusions to Buddhism, all of them formal in nature.

There is more at stake here than simple over-generalization. Barbour explicitly acknowledges the reality of other religions, yet nowhere does religion's dialogue with science become interreligious. In fact, he identifies "religious pluralism" as one of the five great challenges facing Christianity today, which include "science as a method, a new view of nature, a new context for theology, and threats to the environment." He is quick to pick up on the challenge that follows logically from this claim: "to explore the place of religion in an age of science and to present an interpretation of Christianity that is responsive both to the biblical faith and to contemporary science."[43] In the end, however, the gap between "the place of religion" and "the interpretation of Christianity" remains unfilled.

A similar criticism may be raised against the work of Ted Peters, who has taken a leading role in the dialogue between theology and the natural sciences, notably in connection with the theological and ethical problems raised by the birth of Dolly the cloned sheep in 1996. Unfortunately, his generalizations regarding "religion" are as misplaced as Barbour's. After presenting models for the religion-science dialogue, he concludes in tell-tale fashion:

> Theologians, who reflect rationally on their religious faith, are naturally drawn
> to the rigors of scientific discourse. Theologians recognize a kindred spirit in
> scientists in pursuit of discovery, new knowledge, and expansion of our shared

worldview. Like cheerleaders on the grid iron, theologians applaud scientific touchdowns....

By and large, theologians find themselves engaged in worldview construction. Presuming both hypothetical consonance and critical realism, theologians draw the most comprehensive picture of reality imaginable. They try to locate everything in the physical and historical world in relationship to the one gracious God who is both creator and redeemer. Confirmed scientific knowledge contributes much to what goes into this picture. We have referred above to this model as *theology of nature.*

The never-ending construction of this worldview benefits from the dialogue between theology and science, as we have seen. Relying on the bridge metaphor, science sends a great deal of traffic toward the religious side of the bridge. Might traffic go the other direction? Yes. This dialogue may have moments when the theologian offers an insight that could lead the laboratory scientist toward a progressive research program, toward an advance in scientific knowing. When traffic flows both directions, we have *creative mutual interaction.*[44]

Peters's working assumption is that religion and science, although initially separate, can be integrated theologically without forfeiting the distinct qualities of each. This is evident from his choice of terms: "bridge," "interaction," "consonance." The integration he elaborates is not between religion and science but between Christian theology posing as religion and science. The goal is to fuse the scientific view of nature with the Christian view of nature as the creation of "one gracious God." His model of "dialogue leading to creative mutual interaction" rests on the premise that "God's objective action breaks no natural laws"[45] and leads him to conclude that "theologians can applaud scientific touchdowns" like "cheerleaders on the gridiron." Whenever the creative hands of God interact with the players, they do so without breaking the rules of the game. This kind of "religious naturalism" or "theistic naturalism"[46] amounts to a theology of the natural world grounded in the historical revelation of the Bible and confirmed in personal experience: "God acts in nature" but "does not disparage or neglect the natural order.[47]

In effect, the "integration" of religion and science functions as a kind of litmus paper for testing the truth of theological claims. Dip into the solution and you will be able to determine whether the views concentrated there accord with the faith or oppose it. The problem, of course, is that because theology has been in control of the religion-science amalgam from the start, its use as a standard of truth is seriously compromised. If the rules of engagement are slanted towards the Christian faith to begin with, the dialogue will end up telling us more about what theology thinks it knows about religion and science than about religion and science themselves.[48] What appear to be the voices of religion and science in dialogue are actually the voice of a theological ventriloquist.

As the above example show, theological assumptions can corrupt the dialogue between religion and science from the ground up. As we have been insisting, Christianity's dialogue with religion cannot be separated from its dialogue with science. The two are interactive and interdependent not as separate activities but as overlapping elements that are always present in Christianity's encounter with the world, whether we are aware of it or not. When the left hand of the theologian dialogues with religions, it may not realize that at the same time the right hand is in dialogue with science. The reason is rather simple. Christianity's dialogue with religion-science does not take place in some airy realm of abstraction, but in the thick of things where faith is lived. When it comes to dialogue, faith cannot be bracketed in an act of methodological epoché or scientific detachment. By the same token, faith cannot allow its pursuit of truth to land it in a *sacrificium intellectus* in the name of fair-mindedness or epistemological humility. In the dialogue, the full horizon is present to the life of faith at once. Religion and science are not separate topics to be taken up in proper order and only integrated later.

Think for a moment what happens when you take a drink of water. We know from chemistry that water is a combination of oxygen and hydrogen, but if we first drink the hydrogen molecules and then the oxygen molecules, we have not actually drunk water at all. The same may be said of the theological experiment of separating actual, living faith from religion and science in order to deal first with one and then with the other. Those who have engaged in such encounters may be convinced they are performing an important service, but the fruits of their efforts come at the cost of artificially dismantling the reality of religion-science into its component parts.

Theological reflection on Christianity's dialogue with science today must begin from the elementary fact that the faith that seeks contact with other religions is the very same faith that seeks a better understanding of science and its meaning for religion. Insofar as the Christian faith is shaped *simultaneously* by the dialogue with religion and the dialogue with science, their overlap is essential to the self-understanding of Christianity. (Regarding the tendency of Christian theology to monopolize the agenda of these dialogues, we shall have more to say in the following section.)

The two dialogues overlap not only in time but also in value. Neither takes precedence over the other. To borrow a term from Heidegger, they shape Christian faith *equiprimordially*. Just as an individual's state-of-mind, understanding, and discourse have a commensurate share in the existential constitution of *Dasein*, such that none of them can be absorbed or superseded by any other,[49] so, too, religion and science constitute fundamental and irreducible elements for understanding reality. Heidegger's English translator, John Macquarrie, coined the term "equiprimordial" to translate *gleich-ursprünglich* with its sense of "existing together as equally fundamental *ab initio*," or "equally original." Things related in this matter are ontologically and temporally distinct, yet inseparable from one another. They are also elemental in the sense that they do not derive from a common *tertium quid*. In short, the overlap in theology's dialogue with religion and science rests on a mutual interpenetration in which neither can claim precedence as to time or value.

Carl Friedrich von Weizsäcker, the German physicist, philosopher, and Nobel Laureate, has likened the mutual entailment of religion and science to the two halves of a circle;

> Natural science and humanistic disciplines appear to me like two half-circles. They ought to be joined in such a way that they combine to form a full circle, and this circle ought then to be followed round fully, many times. By this I mean:
>
> On the one hand, man is himself a being of nature. Nature is older than man. Man has come out of nature and is subject to her laws. An entire science, medical science, is successfully engaged in studying man as a part of nature, with the methods of natural science. In this sense, the humanistic disciplines presuppose natural science.
>
> On the other hand, natural science is itself made by man and for man, and is subject to the conditions of every intellectual and material work of man. Man is older than natural science. Nature had to be so that there could be man— man had to be so that there could be concepts of nature. It is possible as well as necessary to understand natural science as a part of man's intellectual life. In this sense, natural science presupposes the humanistic disciplines.[50]

Insofar as we are a part of nature, we need the tools of the natural sciences to understand what it is to be a human being. To accept ourselves as objects of scientific research is to presuppose the principles of science. At the same time, those principles are conventions of our own making. As important as the natural sciences are for our self-understanding, they are not the whole of it. Some account has also to be made of the other "half-circle" where the scientific method arose. This is the purview of human sciences, where religion comes into the picture.

The synthesis of these two halves of understanding the human is less like an uroboros swallowing its own tail than what von Weizsäcker calls a "circling" (*Kreisgang*)," namely the reciprocal explanation of nature through knowledge and of knowledge through the history of nature."[51] Understanding the whole (nature) and understanding the part (human being) orbit the same reality. Together, the natural sciences and the human sciences constitute a kind of Heideggerian "hermeneutical circle." For Heidegger, we recall, all understanding requires a structural anticipation that he calls "fore-understanding" or "fore-project." Unlike the fallacy of circular reasoning in which a conclusion is already contained in the premise of an argument, advance understanding is a condition for the possibility of all interpretation and belongs to "the ontological structure of understanding."[52]

The notion of the hermeneutical circle also implies that the interpreter belongs to the object of interpretation. Gadamer speaks in this connection of the "principle of the history of effect," by which he means to highlight the subsequent impact that a text and the history of its study has on its interpreters, consciously or otherwise. Any attempt to understand the full history of a text in this sense can never be separated from the way in which that history shapes the one who does the understanding. The two form a circle. To understand is not to possess an object of knowledge but to be caught up in a process of "hermeneutical circulation." As an individual thrown into a particular set of historical circumstances, my every attempt to understand the world is also a "projection" of myself and my "potentiality-for being".[53] Understanding and self-understanding entail one another. Gadamer describes it this way:

> In fact history does not belong to us; we belong to it. Long before we understand ourselves through the process of self-examination, we understand ourselves in a self-evident way in the family, society, and state in which we live. The

focus of subjectivity is a distorting mirror. The self-awareness of the individual is only a flickering in the closed circuits of historical life. That is why the prejudices of the individual, far more than his judgments, constitute the historical reality of his being.[54]

Von Weizsäcker describes this process of hermeneutical circling in terms of the relationship between human being and nature:

> We are children of nature. Nature is older than humanity, but humanity is older than science. This fact allows philosophy to take a circular path (*Kreisgang*) that was not open to classical metaphysics. Classical philosophy understood the human being as knower and nature as the known. It did not take into account the natural history of human knowledge.[55]

To pick up where we left off, when Christian theology enters into dialogue with other religions or with the natural sciences, it does so within a worldview shaped jointly by religious pluralism and the scientific mindset. The searching, existential questions with which religion and science confront the self-understanding of the Christian faith today are not an assault from without. They belong simultaneously and equiprimordially to the same historical reality within which theology must struggle to give an intelligible yet faithful account of the Christian tradition. The challenge, in von Weizsäcker's words, could not be clearer:

> What will our theology look like if we try... to remain honest to history and at the same time honest to nature? And at what point do we need to sacrifice the pride we take in that honesty for the sake of a greater experience?[56]

Why buddhism and biology?

At this point in the discussion, we need to be realistic. Unless we are able to make the transition from theoretical questions of methodology and interpretation to the actual practice of bringing theology, religion, and science into dialogue, our arguments have no hope of producing concrete results. Obviously, it is impossible for theology in general to dialogue with religion and science in general. We cannot dialogue with "religion" in the abstract any more than we can dialogue with all the religions of the world at once. The same holds true of "science" and the wide range of disciplines that term covers. Granted, ambiguity and abstractness are necessary for examining the logic and principles of interpretation. But my aim in these pages is different. Simply put, I would like to approach theology's dialogue with religion and science as an adventure in learning—more specifically, learning from the Buddhist perspective on reality and from the worldview of biological science.

My choice of Buddhism as a *Sitz im Leben* hardly needs defending. Its religious teachings, practices, and spiritualities have grounded the cultures of Asia for millennia and continue to spread across the globe in our own times. Among the rich variety of Buddhist schools, I will focus in particular on Zen and Huayan teachings because of their connection with popular religiosity in Asia. Furthermore, rather than treat these Buddhist teachings in one of their traditional forms, I will center my attention on modern Japanese Buddhist philosophy as represented in the thought of Nishitani Keiji, a leading figure of the Kyoto School, a group of twentieth-century philosophers who distinguished themselves by adapting the Christian philosophy of the West to the logic and questions of their own cultural and religious heritage.

The choice of biology has to do more directly with its formative role in our contemporary worldview. A variety of biological disciplines, among them sociobiology and cognitive biology, have applied their methods and theories to religious phenomena. In addition, since the Darwinian revolution biology has taken over from physics and astronomy as the greater challenge to theology. DNA has taken over from the atom as the defining icon of our age and has had a profound affected on the way we view reality. As the historian of science William Dampier wrote nearly a century ago:

> In the great advance which marked the nineteenth century, it was not the vast development of physical knowledge, and still less the enormous superstructure of industry raised on that knowledge, which most effectually widened man's horizon and led to one more revolution in his ways of thought. The point of real interest shifted from astronomy to geology, and from physics to biology and the phenomena of life. The hypothesis of natural selection, which first gave an acceptable basis for the old idea of evolution, carried the human mind over the next long stage of its endless journey, with Darwin as the Newton of biology—the central figure of nineteenth-century thought.[57]

After Ptolemy's geocentric cosmology had been dethroned by the Copernican revolution, an anthropocentric view of the natural world stepped in to take its place. The idea of the "great chain of being"(*scala naturae*) that the West had inherited from Aristotle lent support to Christianity's belief in the human being as the crown of divine creation. The entire structure of reality was laid out in a strict hierarchy. At the top stood the realm of the provident, creator God; below it followed multiple orders that included the realms of angels, human beings, animals, plants, and so forth, all the way down to the lowest domains occupied by entities considered inanimate, like stones and mushrooms. The entire structure was designed by God to maintain an absolute disconnect between one level and another.[58] Any attempt to invert the order was censured as the hybris of "playing God." Darwinian revolution deconstrucuted the system and did away with the ontological distinction among the levels. This marked the collapse of the Christian worldview based on faith in creation. The influence of biology on Christian theology was like a force aimed at liberating people once and for all from the "spiritual universe" they had previously inhabited,[59] including the vestiges that had remained in the wake of the Copernican revolution.

Unlike many physicists, who continue to indulge metaphysical speculations about the origins of the universe (for example, von Weizsäcker rejects the idea of employing the Big Bang theory as "a myth of creation for the century of the atomic bomb"),[60] biologists tended to be more brazen in their criticism of religion. Indeed, among all the sciences, none has touched the heart of the Christian faith as deeply as biology. Darwin's theory excluded from the flow of evolution the possibility of any metaphysical and teleological meaning to human existence. As Hans Jonas pointed out, the philosophical implications of Darwinian theory are apparent from its negation of Platonism and the idea of a human "essence," which in turn gave birth to nihilism.[61]

If, as Daniel Dennett argues, "there is no such thing as philosophy-free science," then the Darwinian revolution "is both a scientific and a philosophical revolution, and neither revolution could have occurred without the other."[62] Since Darwin, biology has insisted with increasing vigor that it is able to explain the nature of the human being without the use of traditional metaphysics. The French biochemist Jacques Monod put it this way:

Biology occupies a position among the sciences at once marginal and central. Marginal because-the living world constituting but a tiny and very "special" part of the universe—it does not seem likely that the study of living beings will ever uncover general laws applicable outside the biosphere. But if the ultimate aim of the whole of science is indeed, as I believe, to clarify man's relationship to the universe, then biology must be accorded a central position, since of all the disciplines it is the one that endeavors to go most directly to the heart of the problems that must be resolved before that of "human nature" can even be framed in other than metaphysical terms. Consequently no other science has quite the same significance for man; none has already so heavily contributed to the shaping of modern thought, profoundly and definitively affected as it has been in every domain-philosophical, religious, political-by the advent of the theory of evolution.[63]

From this self-assertive position as a scientist, Monod argued for disposing of the "old covenant" with its faith in creation and hylozoism, and replacing it with an "ethics of knowledge." By that he meant an ethic of atheistic humanism and biological iconoclasm that stood ready prepared to topple any idol that hindered the exercise of free will grounded in exact knowledge of the world and human beings.

Perhaps the most decisive blow the Darwinian revolution struck against the Christan worldview was its dismissal of teleological thinking. Belief in creation assumes a higher, provident will with a purpose for the world. Darwin saw no need for such belief. Despite the title of his book, *The Origin of Species*, Darwin has no intention of explaining the origin of anything. His concern was with change over time on the assumption that neither *arche* nor *telos* is involved. He viewed each species as a "variation" produced by chance through adaptation its surroundings. He saw no grounds for arguing from the coincidental rise of variations to an original, or "true" species "independently created." In his view, it is simply impossible to "define, or even conjecture, which are the created forms of life, and which are those produced by secondary laws."[64] As a result, "the naturalist loses his best guide in determining whether to rank doubtful forms as varieties or species"[65] and lacks any criteria for distinguishing species from variations other than a seemingly tautological judgment that variation is the "true cause" (*vera causa*) of variation.

Christian faith was quick to recognize the consequences of Darwin's theory, as Bertrand Russel points out:

As often happens, the theologians were quicker to perceive the consequences of the new doctrine than were its advocates, most of whom, though convinced by the evidence, were religious men, and wished to retain as much as possible of their former beliefs.[66]

For the eminent German biologist Ernst Mayr, Darwin offered good reason for Christianity to take up the dialogue with biology more urgently than with any other scientific discipline. His uncommon boldness and honesty as an intellectual in the Victorian age led him to raise "the most profound questions about our origins that have ever been asked, and as a devoted and innovative scientist he provided brilliant, often world-shattering answers."[67]

To appreciate the full force of biology on the Christian way of life and thought, however, there is no need to return to nineteenth-century evolutionary theory. One need only recall the global uproar in 1997 surrounding a sheep named Dolly, whom Ian Wilmut, an English biologist and embryologist at Roslin Institute, had cloned in his laboratory. The debate has since spilled over into biotechnological and bioethical issues such as birth control, abortion, euthanasia, brain death, organ transplantation, homosexuality, transgender surgery, and indeed human cloning. At the center of everything is the question what constitutes life, which can no longer be addressed without involving the methods and results of research in biology.

A TIME TO START

Before taking up the dialogue with religion and science together, we should acknowledge previous attempts along the same lines, rare as they are. The work of John Hick and Paul Ingram comes immediately to mind, both of whom have made creative contributions to interreligious dialogue and the self-understanding of religious pluralism. We have good reason to expect clues from them regarding a theological encounter with science based on the theological encounter with religions.

I begin with Hick's book *The New Frontier of Religion and Science: Religious Experience, Neuroscience, and the Transcendent*, in which he takes up the relation between religious phenomena as a spiritual experience and the materialistic approach to these phenomena by neuroscience. As one of the foremost pioneers in the theology of religious pluralism, Hick shares the concerns of other theologians and scholars of the human sciences seeking to defend the existence of a spiritual reality and possibility of genuine religious experience from the reductionist assault of brain science. In his view, "religion's fundamental debate is with materialism, or physicalism, which is incompatible with the existence of any ultimate transcendent reality such as the religions point to in their different ways." In particular, Hick points to recent claims from the neurosciences that the human mind is "at most a mysterious temporary by-product of the functioning of the brain." Accordingly,

> religious experience is not, in any of its forms, an authentic awareness of a reality transcending the material universe—for according to materialism there can be no such reality—but merely a reflection of physical events in the brain within the seamless causal continuity of the natural world.[68]

Whatever the case may be in Christianity, the larger question is whether "a reality transcending the material universe" is a necessary condition for speaking of experiences or phenomena as *religious*. The fact is, in Japan—as in much of East Asia where the dominant spiritual context is Buddhist—the science-religion dialogue is carried out more effectively without the idea of God or some transcendent reality beyond the material universe. Where the Christian faith sees a divine creator behind the world, Buddhism sees the co-arising of all things according to the laws of *karma*. In such an apparently "mechanical" worldview, the existence of a personal God is superfluous for explaining the origin of things and the reality of suffering. Rather,

> in order to arrive at the goal of extinguishing desire from the mind, Buddhism, which from the beginning has understood materials and spirits from a godless, mechanical worldview, tried to know which law the mind should follow. Science has investigated the matter; Buddhism has inquired into the mind. To improve the mind, we have to know its structure precisely. As long as there is no absolute one moving freely, the mind moves by strictly following its very own law. In order to rid oneself of desires, a Buddhist should be well aware of the law of the mind and use it correctly.[69]

On the one hand, Hick is prepared to acknowledge various extraordinary or paranormal experiences induced by epilepsy, drugs, or brain surgery that bear resemblance to the disruption of normal brain functions found in religious experiences. On the other hand, he wants to keep such phenomena distinct from authentic religious experiences, which are characterized by personal or social transformation: "You will know them by their fruits" (Matt 7:20).[70]

Hick is not unaware of the controversy surrounding the mind/brain problem, but he insists that brain science can only deal with the brain as matter, not the unique meaning that the mind and heart generate under the influence of the brain:

> I conclude that the relationship between brain and consciousness is like that between two dancers who always move together, but sometimes with one and sometimes the other taking the lead. This involves a defense of non-compatibilist free will, which hinges finally upon the performative contradiction involved in claiming, as a fully determined mind/brain, to know or rationally believe that one is a fully determined mind/brain. Not only all personal relationships but all creative work in literature, painting, music, architecture, and equally in all the great scientific advances, presupposes a significant degree of intellectual and physical freedom.[71]

Hick combines various types of religious experience under the general category "religious experience," all of which he presupposes require the existence of transcendent reality. To justify his position, he appeals time and again to his "pluralist hypothesis,"[72] namely, that the varieties of religious experience represents different cultural and religious paths ways to a single ultimate reality "transcending the material universe." Absent such a hypothesis, Hick believes, true religious experience is impossible.

In effect, Hick is drawing on a time-worn tradition of appealing to theistic or monotheistic beliefs to "defend" religion from the "challenge" of science. It is the same strategy he employs in defense of the universality of the theistic Christian faith from the challenge of the non-theistic religions. He sees no difficulty in transplanting the "pluralist hypothesis" from an interreligious setting to the dialogue with religion and science. We shall leave further discussion and evaluation of his pluralist hypothesis for Chapter 4, where we take up the question of a theology for religious pluralism.

Within the limits of his pluralist hypothesis, Hick follows a rather standard Christian approach to science with little concern for the way other religions question science. Rather like Whitehead's "fallacy of misplaced concreteness" turned inside out, Hick's failure is one of misplaced generalization. It grants Christian theology a monopoly that effectively excludes the form and content of Buddhism's encounter with science.

Paul Ingram's work is like Hick's in that he endeavors to draw a straight line from interreligious dialogue and to the dialogue of religion with science and considers brain science the most recent and radical challenge to religion. He grounds his idea of a "trialogue" of Christianity and Buddhism with science on the claim that "the goal of Buddhist-Christian conceptual dialogue with the natural sciences is the creative transformation of both traditions."[73] In particular, he poses the question, "What, if anything, would Buddhist-Christian dialogue with the natural sciences add to current Buddhist-Christian encounter?"[74]

Ingram spends a great deal of his book describing and comparing Christian and Buddhist understandings of scientific discoveries in cosmology, brain science, and the cognitive science of religion. In addition to reviewing Ian Barbour's typology of the Christian encounter with science and José Cabezón's typology of the Buddhist models for interpreting scientific worldviews, he offers an overview of Christian and Buddhist responses to evolutionary biology. His chapters on the the dialogue with cognitive science and the structure of the Buddhist-Christian-science dialogue are the most interesting for our purposes here.

That said, I find his proposal of a Big Bang theology to adopt the "current scientific origin narrative" in order to "clarify and transform religious creation myths" and "give expression to religious experiences and convictions that are already present in most religious communities" something of an interreligious embarrassment. The logic of his move from identifying Big Bang theory as "a common origin story that is available to be remythologized by most religious traditions in terms of their own specific history and practices" to the conclusion that therefore "scientific cosmology is a place of meeting for the world's religions" escapes me. However, as von Weizsäcker noted, it is questionable whether the Big Bang theory can simply take over the role of Christianity's traditional story of creation. That aside, Ingram's approach to science remains biased strongly in the direction of Christianity. In the end, neither he nor Hick seem to offer hope of integrating the Christian dialogue with Buddhism and with natural science might into a new paradigm.

Ingram was aware that his attempts to rethink the religion-science dialogue from the perspective of religious pluralism, like Hick's, were a work in progress. In that sense, his concluding *Postscript* marks the very point of our departure:

> Accordingly, the final conclusion of this book is one that is still in process.... The most important theological tasks confronting thinking Christians are (1) dialogue with the world's religious traditions, and (2) dialogue with the natural sciences.... Both tasks are interdependent and demand intentionally bringing the natural science into interreligious dialogue as a third partner. This has not as yet happened in any systematic fashion in any specific interreligious dialogue, including contemporary Buddhist-Christian dialogue. It's time to start.[75]

2

Placing Christianity in History, Humanity in Nature

One swallow, it is said, does not make a summer. Nor, I would add, is a single fallacy reason enough to dispense with an entire argument and its conclusions. Like the swallow that gives us an idea what to expect, there have been harbingers already from the first half of the last century signaling that the time has come for theology to engage seriously with religion and science. Whatever the failures so far, the time is still upon us.

I draw attention to two early voices heralding the dialogue. The first is a relatively long essay by Ernst Troeltsch (1865–1923), originally prepared as a lecture at Oxford University, "The Place of Christianity among World Religions." The other is a book by Max Scheler (1874–1928) that deals with the "place" of human beings in the natural world, *The Human Place in the Cosmos*.

As we see from their respective titles, these two contemporary German thinkers were concerned with where to place Christianity in the history of religions and where to place human beings in the history of the cosmos respectively. Why such a question? And why at that time? Clearly Troeltsch and Scheler were both aware that the place of Christianity and the place of the human were in peril, or at least not as self-evident as they had once been. Theologians in increasing numbers were awakening to the fact the ground was shifting under their feet. The tradition of beliefs and the institutions that upheld them were at a turning point, after which Christianity would no longer be able to sustain its privilege position as the unique and absolute revelation of God for the salvation of the whole world. For their part, philosophers working within a civilization shaped by Christian doctrine and scriptures were beginning to realize that the status of human beings as the "crown of creation" and the worldview built on that belief was coming to an end.

That Troeltsch and Scheler should both have been preoccupied with the *placing* of Christianity and humans at the same time is more than mere coincidence. It is symbolic of an age that was shaking off the last vestiges of faith from the pursuit of science. The study of the natural world and the study of religion were no longer under obligation to the Christian metaphysic of the past. Like anthropology, theology was being asked to rethink its subject matter and its methods from the ground up in order to respond to the ascendancy of historicism and naturalism, the identical twins in control of ways of thought of the modern world.

CHRISTIANITY'S PLACE IN HISTORY: ONE FAITH IN MANY FAITHS

The historical method

In surveying the variety of Christian approaches to other religions through history, Paul Knitter states forthrightly that "much of what we feel concerning religious pluralism is mirrored in Ernst Troeltsch."[1] It is difficult to overstate the archetypal importance of Troeltsch's theology in shaping the way later generations were to interpret the religious wealth of humankind. At the same time, a closer look at his thinking and perspective exposes important limitations in his theology of religions.

More than any theologian of his time, and perhaps more than most since, Troeltsch understood that the essence and value of Christianity are a function of its place in the broader history of religions. He recognized the serious problems facing traditional Christianity for its claims to an exclusive and decisive role in the salvation of humanity, regardless of the rest of religious history. As Wolfhardt Pannenberg has noted, Troeltsch deserves to be remembered for confronting modern theology with its most fundamental questions and challenges.[2] In a lengthy essay on the importance of history for theology, Pannenberg argues that the "dialectical theology" of Karl Barth and Rudolf Bultmann needs to be replaced by a new paradigm that understands Christianity from the perspective of the history of religion. Troeltsch's theology, he suggests, offers just such an alternative paradigm for a theology that has "awakened from the dream of a *kerygma*."[3] If our aim is to grasp the faith in its entirety, restricting attention to Christianity's account of its own affairs is counter-productive. We can agree here with Knitter that Troeltsch was far ahead of his time in acknowledging the reality of religious pluralism.

Pannenberg also refers to the influence of Troeltsch on the late writings of Paul Tillich with regard to the meaning of the history of religion for theology. Tillich's famous lecture on "The Significance of Religious History for the Systematic Theologian" comes to mind at once. By the end of his life, Tillich was persuaded that any positive and critical evaluation of the universal truth of Christianity can only be made by understanding Christianity as one faith among many in human history. In *Christianity and the Encounter of the World's Religions* we see the eagerness with which he turned to the study of comparative religions for guidance in reconstructing the theological system he had built on the pillars of Western philosophical ontology.[4] Here again, Pannenberg insists us, Tillich's fascination with the universality and historicity of Christian revelation, can be traced back to Troeltsch, whom Tillich explicitly referred to as "my own teacher."[5] In a 1924 essay on Troeltsch's place in intellectual history, Tillich identified the core of Troeltsch's theological struggle in "the tension between the absolute and the relative," which he "saw as crucial and experienced with a passion":

> This is demonstrated not only in the dynamism of his thinking, which took him further than he had ever gone before, and beyond his previous scope of inquiry, but also by the ambivalence of the fate that had placed him between theology as a symbol of his desire for the absolute, on the one hand, and philosophy as an expression of the conditionality and infinite variety of the actual world, on the other. And here, too, it was fate that inclined him towards the relative in the struggle to resolve this contradiction.[6]

The tension between the absolute and the relative in Troeltsch, which constellated in the conflicting method of theology and philosophy, represents the starting point for Troeltsch's approach to other religions. It also showed the limits to his theological reflection on other religions and his evaluation of them. Troeltsch did not learn from other religions through direct contact but through the extension and application of traditional dichotomies like grace and law, faith and reason, gospel and culture. Other religions were merely objects for theological reflection in general and abstract terms; dialogue was little more than intellectual ventriloquism.

The battle lines between the absolute and the relative were later redrawn to a face-off between Christianity's absoluteness as the revelation of God and its relativity as one particular historical phenomenon among a plurality of religious traditions. As Tillich pointed out, by temperament Troeltsch inclined toward the relative. His "uncompromising spirit" as a thinker would not let him simply yield to "doctrinal" claims regarding the absoluteness of Christianity without revising them in a thoroughly "historical" way.

Reflecting on his interest in history, Troeltsch recalled that "from an early age, I have had a deep concern for the historical world, just like Dilthey."[7] From the beginning of the nineteenth century, the study of history had broadened its scope beyond the ancient world and transformed into a rigorous academic discipline. This gave rise to "historicism," which Troeltsch defined as "a way to make our knowledge and thinking,… everything about human beings, their culture and value, thoroughly historical." As the culmination of a process of the "naturalization" of thought that had been underway since the eighteenth century,[8] historicism sought to study all historical phenomena from a radically historical standpoint.

Troeltsch himself was aware that such a historical approach has to rely on probability and analogical thinking. For one thing, no final evaluation is possible while events are still ongoing. For another, historical phenomena are homogeneously interconnected and no single event or cluster of events can be fully understood apart from the others. Given this "fundamental similarity of all historical occurrences," we have no choice but to understand Judeo-Christian history "in analogy to all other histories."[9] What is more, the meaning of the biblical message cannot be comprehended without viewing the history of Christianity in the context of the history of other religions and other cultures. In this sense, Troeltsch likens historicism to natural science in the Middle Ages:

> Because of this it seems from an orthodox standpoint to be rather like the devil. Just like modern natural science it represents a complete revolution in our mode of thinking in comparison with antiquity and the Middle Ages. If modern natural science takes a new posture toward nature, then history takes a

new posture toward the human spirit and its ideal products. The older absolute or dogmatic mode of thinking, which considered specific conditions and ideas as self-evident and thus absolutized them as unchangeable norms, has been displaced by the historical mode, which also deals with what is allegedly self-evident and which considers the widest circles of governing powers as witnesses of the flow of history. It takes hold of law, morality, sociology, political science, and aesthetics in the deepest way and subordinates them to historical points of view and methods.[10]

In the same way that the explanations of natural science reject the working of any supernatural factors, so does historicism exclude whatever transcends the categories of history. The comparison bears directly on our discussion here in the sense that the theological dialogue with other religions takes place on the same dimension as its dialogue with the natural sciences. "History," as Troeltsch was aware, had become central to a theology that could no longer defend the ultimacy and absoluteness of the Christian religion.

Troeltsch took up the question of historicism at length in his 1922 monograph *Historicism and its Problems*. He argued that to base "the historical method" on historicism is to accept that all judgments regarding historical events are relative and that final judgment must be adjourned until the end of time. Thinking about history in the midst of a single, interconnected history precludes us from creating or applying a uniform set of criteria, religious or otherwise. The assessment of historical events is irretrievably plural:

> That is the evident effect of the historical method. It relativizes everything, not in the sense that every gauge of value is ruled out and nihilistic skepticism must result, but in the sense that every moment and every construct of history can be conceived only in connection with others and finally with the whole, that the construction of every gauge of value cannot be based on isolated particulars but only on an overview of the whole.[11]

In Troeltsch's estimation, the historical method or its ancillary history of religions method represented "the much deeper, special point of departure in the shattering of the Christian world view."[12] Faithful to the principles of historicism, he could not allow "a supernatural doctrine of authority" or any ahistorical "dogmatic-apologetic absoluteness" that might be deduced immediately from God. The task of Christian theology in his view was rather to understand the essence and value of the Christian faith historically, that is, as located in the history of religion.

Traditional theological assertions regarding the decisive and indispensable role of Christianity in the salvation of humanity runs into serious opposition when faced with religious traditions outside Christianity. Troeltsch spoke of the "clash between historical reflection and the determination of standards of truth and value,"[13] which ends up depriving Christianity of its claim to absoluteness. Theology has no choice but to rethink the *place* of Christianity among the religions of the world.

The absoluteness of Christianity within the history of religions

Christian theology was understandably agitated by the emergence of historicism. Divine revelation was being stripped of its supernatural and transhistorical characteristics and brought down to earth in the historical world. If revelation is historical, determining whether it is authentic or not requires that it be accessible to human experience. Troeltsch's historicism fed directly into the tendency in modern theology to view revelation from a historical perspective,[14] that is, to speak of God and revelation in terms of human consciousness and activity rather than from fixed ideas of a metaphysical and timeless nature or traces of it hidden in nature. History is not only the locus of working consciousness; it is also its product. Accordingly, all revelation occurs *in* history and also *as* history.

Troeltsch had no doubt that historicism and its effect on theological method would "affect theology the same way it affected everything else—by causing a fundamental transformation in the whole mode of thinking and the basic attitude toward its object."[15] Theology, as we have said, was left no choice but to adjust, which is not to say capitulate. If the history of religions undermines Christianity's self-understanding as the sole universal vehicle for salvation, theology's response should be to embrace it as an internal problem, to redefine the clash with historicism as a transition from absoluteness to the acceptance of Christianity as a historical religion. No revelation, no doctrine was to be exempt from discussion. Troeltsch turned to the internal transformation of theology in his immensely influential book, *The Absoluteness of Christianity and the History of Religions*, of which he was later to write:

The central question here concerned Christianity's right to claim exclusive and absolute validity. I dealt with it in 1902 in *The Absoluteness of Christianity and the History of Religion*. There I took up the unavoidable confrontation between the historical relative and the factual absolute, which my study of the historical method had helped me identify as the core issue for philosophy of history as a whole. The book proved to be the seed for everything that followed. To be sure, the general problem of what constitutes Christianity today was to require closer attention, given the wealth of historical variations and the spiritual crisis of our time.[16]

Troeltsch's critique of Christian exceptionalism rejected the appeal to "absolute self-authentication through the miracles of conversion and the sacraments." Such thinking belonged to an idea of the Church as "a supernatural institution that stands within history but does not derive from history." The overtly apologetic nature of this logic, not to mention the fact that it places Christianity above history, disqualifies it as proof of the absolute claims of Christianity vis-à-vis other religions. For Troeltsch, this way of thinking is utterly incompatible with the "modern idea of history," which "has had a radically dissolving effect on this apologetic structure of thought."[17] Miracles cannot justify assertions of historical fact for the simple reason that they themselves are exempt from historicist and naturalist categories.

Historicism may begin from an awareness of the relativity of all historical events, but this does not mean that it necessarily leads to nihilistic relativism. Troeltsch recognized that every judgment of an historical event contains within it a universal standard of evaluation, even if that event is ongoing and never comes to term. The values by which we measure history are themselves part of the process. Thus, while it is no longer possible to advance the absoluteness of Christianity with doctrinal certitude, its comparison with religions remains open to exploration. In fact, Troeltsch was convinced that it was both possible and necessary to reaffirm the absoluteness of Christianity within the limits of the historical method.

From a historicist perspective, at any given time an abundance of competing religious values is possible. *De facto* the range of viable, concrete religious values is limited by historical circumstances. Judaism, Christianity, Islam, Brahmanism, Buddhism—each of them represents a distinct way of valuing the world. Their influence has waxed and waned from age to age and place to place, but this does not gainsay the importance of religious values for guiding us towards the supernatural from within our particular historical reality. True, there is no transhistorical place we can stand to judge that one religion's values are superior to those of another, no absolute standard for assessing how one measures up relative to another. But for that very reason, there is nothing to prevent us from undertaking the theoretical comparison of religions in the light of "personal, subjective, inner convictions"[18] and testing our comparison in practice.

What is there in practice that might serve as a standard for evaluating one religion relative to another? Troeltsch thought he had found the answer in the concept of person or personality. Christianity holds a place of prominence here for its moral strength and depth of appreciation for the individual person. The Christian Deity is a personal being endowed with free will and the power to raise human beings from out of their natural world and inspire them to behave ethically. Conversely, other religions envision the ultimate as an "impersonal, eternally existing thing" or "an ultimate abstraction from the given and actual."[19] Theirs is a way of "self-redemption" through meditation and training, and lacks the truth, power, and life of the higher world. The contrast between the personal God of Christianity and the impersonal deities in the religions of India, and in particular Buddhism, led Troeltsch to conclude that "Christianity must be understood not only as the culmination point but also as the convergence point of all the developmental tendencies that can be discerned in religion."[20] He explains his position this way:

> Among the great religions, Christianity is in actuality the strongest and most concentrated revelation of personalistic religious apprehension…. Christianity represents the only complete break with the limits and conditions of nature religion. It represents the only depiction of the higher world as infinitely valuable personal life that conditions and shapes all else. It renounces the world, but only to the extent that its superficial, natural significance clings to it and the evil in it has become dominant. It affirms the world to the extent that it is from God and is perceived by men of faith as deriving from and leading to God. And renunciation and affirmation, taken together, disclose the true higher world in a power and independence that are experienced nowhere else.
>
> It is necessary to make a choice between redemption through meditation on Transcendent Being or non-Being and redemption through faithful, trusting participation in the person-like character of God, the ground of all life and of

all genuine value. This is a choice that depends on religious conviction, not scientific demonstration. The higher goal and the greater profundity of life are
found on the side of personalistic religion.[21]

Troeltsch's "personal conviction" of the superiority of a religion pro-
claiming a deity did not entirely override his critical judgment as a scholar.
Nevertheless, there are reasons to be suspicious. For one thing, he seemed
to rely on a rather conventional understanding of "person." The more serious problem is that he felt compelled by his religious convictions to choose
between salvation through meditation on a transcendent being or nothingness, on the one hand, and salvation through an encounter with a personal
God, on the other. In the end, Troeltsch tips his hand to reveal that for him
as an individual and as a theologian, other religions are mere objects exterior
to the Christian faith and never connecting at the core.

The question for us is whether such an approach does justice to the reality of religious pluralism as we understand it today.

One faith in many faiths

Troeltsch's thinking was to undergo one final development. In 1923 he
was invited by Oxford University to deliver a series of lectures in London,
Oxford, and Edinburgh. He intend to take advantage of the opportunity to
smooth relations between Germany and Europe damaged by World War I.
Unfortunately, he died before he could realize his plan. "The Place of Christianity among World Religions," one of the manuscripts he had prepared for
the series, was included in a collection published posthumously by Friedrich von Hügel, who was responsible for Troeltsch's invitation to England.
In his foreword, von Hügel compared the text to Nicholas of Cusa's work
on the "alliance between Christianity and Islam against indifference and
skepticism," *De pace fidei*. After the fall of Constantinople to the Ottaman
empire in 1463, the great cardinal of the German renaissance issued a call for
tolerance between those two Abrahamic religions on the grounds that they
represent different manifestations of one true religion. Troeltsch's lecture is
marked by a similar tone of spiritual depth and intellectual breadth in its
attempt to find a proper place for Christianity among the other religions of
the world. On reading it, von Hügel wrote, it was as if one were breathing

in the "sweetness of humanity rising out of free thinking" and a "gentleness toward non-Christian world religions."[22]

In his lecture, Troeltsch openly acknowledged that his earlier book, *The Absoluteness of Christianity and the History of Religions,* had adopted the historical method to reconfirm the absoluteness of Christianity by comparing it to other world religions. Christianity, he concluded there, marks the point at which these other religions "converge," even if belief in its absoluteness is purely a matter of subjective conviction. Looking back, he admitted that there is much he would change "in terms of theory," but nothing he would take back regarding his "practical standard" for measuring religions.[23] Specifically, he argued that his characterization of Christianity as a "point of convergence" could stand as is with regard to his practice of the faith, but that his logic for justifying it—namely, the historical method—needed to be elevated to a higher dimension on which all suspicion of relativism would be allayed.

He recalled his struggle against two flawed arguments in support of Christianity's absoluteness. The first, the appeal to miracles as a guarantee of the truth of Christian teachings, collapses immediately under the weight of historical and naturalist reason. The second, the Hegelian idea of the advance of history to its final realization in Christianity, reduced the full reality of the tradition to little more than a "theoretical abstraction." Both approaches ignore the lack of historical uniformity and the reality of denominational variance in order to paint Christianity as a single, distinct historical phenomenon. Simply because an individual believer is convinced of the truth of the faith by "deep personal experience and pure conscientiousness" does not exclude the possibility that the same state of mind could take different forms for different groups and under different social and cultural conditions. To be honest to both reason and faith, Troeltsch had to admit that there is no one way to experience "divine life" and that each way demands the same absolute loyalty of its believers. What is more, this "more radical and trans-denominational" insight into the variety of faiths within Christianity itself could then be expanded to "regard the specific kernel of religion as a unique and independent source of life and power.[24]

Broadening the internal perspective on Christianity to include the entire history of religions, Troeltsch then asks, "Can we, then, discover no common goal of religion, nothing at all that is absolute, in the objective sense of constituting a common standard for mankind?" Given his own insistence on the historical particularities of each religion, the question rings rhetorical. And yet, his personal instincts and sense of rationality tell him otherwise. There are, he says, "subjective validities" born of the faith that are "not simply illusions or the products of human vanity. They are products of the impulse towards absolute objective truth, and take effect in the practical sphere under constant critical self-purification and effort at self-improvement." The practical effect they have on people's lives is no mere "illusion." Once again we see his enthusiasm in the struggle to cast a bridge from the radical historicity of faith to personal belief;

> This synthesis cannot as yet be already attained in any one of the historical religions, but that they all are tending in the same direction, and that all seem impelled by an inner force to strive upward towards some unknown final height, where alone the ultimate unity and the final objective validity can lie. And, as all religion has thus a common goal in the Unknown, the Future, perchance in the Beyond, so too it has a common ground in the Divine Spirit ever pressing the finite mind onward towards further light and fuller consciousness, a Spirit which indwells the finite spirit, and whose ultimate union with it is the purpose of the whole many-sided process.[25]

As a possible way to a "synthesis" that is not to be realized in history, Troeltsch was driven at last to the Romantic movement and the mystical tradition, where the "manyness" in history is subsumed into an ultimate "oneness" with the Godhead, where time is reconciled with eternity and the relative with the absolute. Its realization lies in a distant, unknown future wholly beyond the reach of history. And with that, Troeltsch's lifelong spiritual quest for the place of Christianity amidst the multitude of religions in the world comes to its end:

> If each racial group strives to develop its own highest potentialities, we may hope to come nearer to one another. This applies to the great world religions, but it also applies to the various religious denominations, and to individuals in their intercourse with one another. In our earthly experience, the Divine Life is not one, but many. However, to apprehend *the one in the many* constitutes the special character of love.[26]

In a sense, Troeltsch's conclusion was already anticipated by his concern with overcoming historicism's uncompromising attempt to relativize all religious values. From the start, finding a suitable Christian approach to religious pluralism—whether in general or within Christianity—was part of the challenge of the historical method. As Knitter has remarked, this was the heart of the legacy Troeltsch left behind for theologians of later generations. For example, Alan Race's classification of Christian approaches to religions as exclusivism, inclusivism, and pluralism[27] follows directly in Troeltsch's footsteps.

Nevertheless, Troeltsch's theology suffers from inherent limitations that make it difficult for us to embrace it *tout court* today. To begin with, his response to criticisms levelled by the historical method against Christianity was to draw them into the framework of a general conflict between relativism and absolutism that affects all religions. In this way he hoped to maintain the purity and absoluteness of his own faith while acknowledging the relative value of other religions. At first, his rejection of dogmatic and outdated claims of absoluteness led him to relocate the absolute value of Christianity in "personal conviction" without having to compromise the "historical method." Later, as we have seen, he turned to a quasi-mystical understanding of "the One and the many" as a way to resolve the contradiction in "anticipation" of a final resolution beyond history. At no point, however, did he disavow the absolute superiority of Christianity among the many religions that have come and gone throughout human history. As Knitter put it succinctly, "Troeltsch was seeking a platform outside the flux of historical relativities on which he could make such value judgments."[28]

In a word, the inconsistency and tragedy of Troeltsch's life work lay "in the persistent contradiction between his desire for intellectual honesty and his inability to accept the full consequences of his thought."[29] The Japanese theologian Odagaki Masaya takes up the point and suggests a way out of the dilemma in Troeltsch's theology:

> Troeltsch tried to understand the absoluteness of Christianity by adopting historicism and its radicalization of objective thinking. In the end, he came close to understanding the *one as many* [一即多]. But to do so would require a *Kehre* from Western subject-object modes of thinking about Being.[30]

For Odagaki, Troeltsch's argument for the absoluteness of Christianity by comparing it with other world religions throughout history presupposed that those religions exist outside in the historical world, separate his own subjective faith. Furthermore, to synthesize objective fact and subjective truth, Troeltsch had to assume—or as he put it, "anticipate"—a final stage at which the absolute *one* rises above the relative *many* of history. The crucial question, as Odagaki sees it, is whether there might be some other way of overcoming the dichotomy between subjective confession and objective comparison that reflects the reality of living one's faith in a religiously pluralized age. Because he viewed other religions only on an abstract level, Troeltsch's dilemma was in some sense inevitable . Theoretically, he allowed for direct encounter with other religions, but he himself had never been outside of Europe to witness other religions in their native surroundings. Accordingly, his contribution to dialogue among religions was unable to break free of traditional paradigms and face the reality of religion in practice.

Start to finish, Troeltsch's theology of the history of religions was no more than an endeavor to *explain* the phenomenon of religion from the standpoint of Christian faith. As a result, he failed to appreciate the radical consequences of a genuine encounter with other religions, namely, that theology needs to be explained by religion, not the other way around. Hence, the only way for Troeltsch to achieve his goal would have been to invert its basic premise. This is precisely the point of Odagaki's call for a *Kehre* in theological method: to see other religions not as an "object" for theology but as its very essence. To understand another religion, theology needs to turn its questioning of other religions back on itself. We shall have more to say of this in the following chapter.

MANY FAITHS IN ONE FAITH

"Religion" as a theological construct

Ironically, the fact that Troeltsch constructed his idea of religion on theological assumptions prevented him from achieving his goal of giving Christianity its proper place among the world's religions. As the controversy surrounding the birth of religious studies has made clear, the concept of "religion" itself is largely an invention of Western Christianity. The science of religion as an academic discipline grew out of theological faculties in the nineteenth century, where it was subject to the methods and perspectives of Christian theology. Terms like "religion," "the history of religions" (*Religionsgeschichte*), and "world religions" (*Weltreligionen*) owe their coinage and currency to an exclusively Eurocentric understanding of Christianity.[31] The following remarks of Friedrich Heiler confirm the way in which the science of religion had been subordinated to theology:

> We cannot understand religion if we regard it as so much superstition, illusion, and fantasy. Religion has to do with an ultimate reality which reveals itself to us and blesses us. God, revelation, and eternal life are realities for the religious person. In the end, insofar as the science of religion deals not only with psychological and historical phenomena but also with the experience of the other-worldly realities, it is all *theo*logy.[32]

In support of his position, Heiler cited the words that Nathan Söderblom, a Swedish archbishop and one of the founders of the science of religion as a modern discipline, is reported to have spoken on his deathbed: "I know God is alive. I can prove it from the history of religions."

Without the voices of other religions, there can be no interreligious dialogue. So, too, we cannot speak of a "science" of religion if the very definition of the field is under the control of a particular faith. Troeltsch's interest in the history of religion was no doubt a result of his commitment to the historical method. But the "religion" he dealt with was actually a Christian theological construct;

> In theology at the time, we developed our own distinct approach to metaphysics in confrontation with history. Metaphysics and history in constant conflict. From the start, I took a great interest in their relationship, which led me to the science of religion, where their interaction was particularly close. Nevertheless, *the science of religion was theology.*[33]

Troeltsch's dialogue with other religions was guided by his desire to reconstruct Christian theology in the light of the history of religions. The "science of religion" and "history of religions" were Christian creations for proving the existence of God and demonstrating the universal validity of Christian theology. From the time of the Enlightenment in the eighteenth century, Christian theology has had to deal with criticisms from humanism and modern science that concepts like revelation, salvation, creation, and so forth are merely relics of an ancient worldview that is no longer viable. By defining the counters of "religion" and establishing a discipline they called the "history of religions," theologians like Schleiermacher, Troeltsch, and Otto were able to enlist religion as an ally in the battle against theology's detractors. The idea that the world's religions could be studied as historical phenomena rested on the assumption that faith, as a unique way of thinking and being, and theology, as the self-understanding of faith, are universal. In this sense, the science of religion began as an *ancilla theologiae*.

The Enlightenment and its insistence on objective criteria for truth and rejection of the subjective criteria of Christian faith, were the landscape within which modern scientific methods took shape. In their defense, theologians turned to the rich heritage of the world's religions as evidence of a truth beyond the reach of the natural sciences. Religion, they argued, is different (*anders*) from science, and God is absolutely other (*der absolute Andere*) from the material world that science purports to study. In this way, they sought to "convert what were clearly directed specifically against the authority of Christianity... into threats against religion in general."[34]

Faith as a hybrid phenomenon

The critical deconstruction of "religion" as a theological construct demands that we change starting points. Instead of setting out to explain religion in terms of *our* theology, we need to try to explain the Christian faith in terms of the *world's* religions. Without that rational metanoia, neither a general theology of religious pluralism nor an Asian theology of religious pluralism can get off the ground. In other words, we need to stop thinking of religious traditions as objects for theological reflection and accept other faiths as part of the subjectivity of our own religious identity. Thus, for a Christian believer to enter into dialogue with one of the many religions of Asia does not mean to study that religion objectively and come up with a distinctively Christian "take" on its teachings and practices. On the contrary, it means to allow that religion, as a living faith, to inform one's own subjective faith as a Christian. I cannot encounter the religious mind of a Buddhist or Confucian at arm's length. I have to appropriated it into my own faith, which is only possible, as Odagaki suggests, through a *conversion* in the way I understands what it means to be a Christian. Genuine dialogue with the faith of another does not take place outside of or parallel to Christian faith but directly *within* it.

Among the many questions confronting theology today as it tries to finds its proper place in a religiously plural world is that of "multiple belonging." The affront to the absoluteness of the Christian faith could not be more momentous, yet it reflects the reality in which more and more believers find themselves. No amount of abstract speculation on the doctrinal consequences of belonging to more than one religion can prevent the question from being asked, Does the Christian faith, by its very nature, exclude belief in other faiths? So long as theology sees itself as a discipline for understanding the faith, it must begin from the questions that believers put to it, not the other way around. And so long as theology accepts the reality of other religions, it cannot simply reduce them without remainder to its own categories.

Throughout its history, Christian identity has been shaped not only by distancing itself from other modes of thought and belief but also by assimilating elements from them. This is not to say that theology is working towards some final, definitive configuration. Quite the opposite, the mutual influence of Christianity and its surroundings, including its interactions with other religious ways, should be a permanent feature of all theological reflection. We may compare it to what Monica C. Coleman, writing from an African-American religious context, calls a "Womb Circle," that is to say, a *place* where new ways of understanding and practicing the faith comes to birth. There is an obvious "incommensurability"[35] between her paradigm and older ways of thinking of non-Christian religions as outside the faith. To position Christianity within the womb circle of religions is to redefine the development of the faith as the collaboration of many faiths dwelling in a single faith. Coleman is critical of theologians of religious pluralism like Knitter and Hick who question the possibility of multiple belonging:

> The Womb Circle draws attention to at least one problematic assumption in all the conversations about religious pluralism as they [*sc.*, John Hick and Paul Knitter] tend to occur in the academy and in wider public life. The assumption is that each of us identifies him or herself in one discrete religious tradition and then interacts with those other people who also identify themselves as members or adherents of a different and yet also single and discrete religious tradition. The Womb Circle exists as part of a larger African American religious tradi-

tion that illustrates that this assumption is, in many contexts, fallacious. That is, there are individuals—indeed entire communities—that do not function as members of a single unitary religious tradition. There are individuals—indeed entire communities—that *live and function as members of multiple religious traditions simultaneously.* In these contexts, conversations about religious plurality are not just between discrete faith traditions and communities—about being interreligious—but rather about being multi-religious. And while examples may be found outside of African American religions, I believe that African American religions are distinctively qualified to discuss this multi-religious existence because this it is not a new phenomenon or realization for African American religions. Rather, multi-religious living is woven into the history and reality of African American religions.[36]

As Coleman insists, all religions are by nature essence "syncretic," and, as a result, "pluralistic dialogue and interaction" among religions represents an authentic form of "religious practice."[37] Coleman's criticism of Paul Knitter may need adjusting in light of his later autobiographical work, *Without Buddha I Could not be a Christian*, where he acknowledges the "hybrid" nature of faith as something positive:

> Our religious self, like our cultural or social self, is at its core and in its conduct a hybrid. That means that our religious identity is not purebred, it is hybrid. It is not singular, it is plural. It takes shape through an ongoing process of standing in one place and stepping into other places, of forming a sense of self and then expanding or correcting that sense as we meet other selves. There is no such thing as a neatly defined, once-and-for-all identity. Buddhists, indeed, are right: there is no isolated, permanent self. We are constantly changing and we are changing through the hybridizing process of interacting with others who often are very different from us.[38]

If, in sympathy with Knitter's lifelong quest of religious identity, we can accept his conclusion that religious identity by nature is "syncretic" and "hybrid," the theological burden and personal anxiety of trying to justify Christian exclusivism ceases to be a serious obstacle to multiple religious belonging. Quite the contrary, religious faith and identity open themselves naturally to multiple religious traditions wherever we find "the ontological condition of two or more religions partially constituting the self."[39] I agree with J. R. Hustwit's support of multiple belonging by referring to Gadamer's hermeneutical insight that understanding is realized through the "history of effect" and a fusion of horizons. The Buddhist idea of the self as emerging co-dependently may be seen to include the place a religious plural self plays in the construction of the self. We will come back to this issue in Chapter 5, where we will argue that religious identity in a given faith is grounded in an interpenetrating, multilayered world of faiths—in Huayan Buddhist terms, a *dhātu* of faiths.

Our usual approach to understanding complex realities is to analyze them into their composite parts. This is literally what "abstraction" means. Take the color violet. Only in abstraction is it a combination of the colors red and blue. In nature, it is simply violet. In the attempt to capture religious identity in the concrete, Robert Wuthnow characterized its form in the United States at the end of the twentieth century as a "patchwork quilt" composed of several distinct traditions at the same time.[40] But this is only part of the picture. A faith based in intrinsic hybridity has also to include the organic, cincuminsessional, and mutual influence of multiple religions in a single faith. That is to say, multiple religious belonging does not merely mean that various religious ideas and practices are stitched together in such a way that the sum of the patches comprise one, unified picture. Rather, several religious traditions are constellated in a given faith such that each interacts with the others. This give-and-take is the new horizon against which received tradition is to be reinvented.

Jan Van Bragt describes the phenomenon of multiple religious belonging as a proper and accepted mode of religiosity in Asia. In Japan, for example, people are accustomed to living in several religious worlds at the same time without regard for their competing belief systems.[41] I believe we can develop this way of thinking into the kind of general definition of multiple religious belonging called for in a religiously plural world. This, in turn, would lead us to pursue models of interreligious dialogue in which theology would undergo a conversion (*Kehre*) from its former way of looking on other faiths as objects for reflection and interpretation to an acceptance of them as part of the subjective faith of the theologian. For this reason, Van Bragt insists that the defining mark of the age of interreligious dialogue and religious pluralism is the fact that "purely intrareligious problems—themes that are relevant for one religion only—have ceased to exist."[42] Once we acknowledge that faith is more than one block of teachings competing with others for the position of superiority, and accept that understanding one faith entails understanding other faiths through dialogue, it is a short step to seeing multiple religious belonging as a condition for the possibility of doing theology today.

From this perspective, Van Bragt goes on to survey the theological responses in Japan to the Christian-Buddhist dialogue. To begin with, he singles out three principle motives for Japanese theologians to engage in dialogue with Buddhism. The first of them is a desire for "a more Japanese intellectual underpinning for their Christian faith," something better suited to their Eastern-Japanese bodies than the ill-fitting Western robes in which Christianity has clothed their faith.[43] He calls this the "inculturation motive" and cites as a concrete example the writings of Endō Shūsaku, a twentieth-century Japanese Catholic novelist who struggled to transform Western expressions of Christian faith dominant in Japan into a way of belief rooted in a different religious soil. Faith in God as a merciful mother who mirrors the "mercy of the Buddha" is an example of what Endō had in mind.[44] I cite a passage from his 1966 novel *Silence* in which he describes Japanese spirituality as a "swamp" that absorbs, "twists, and changes" everything Christianity tries to plant in it:

> Father, you were not defeated by me.... You were defeated by this swamp of Japan.... Previously I have asked the question to other fathers: What is the difference between the mercy of the Christian God and that of the Buddha? For in Japan salvation is from the mercy of the Buddha upon whom people depend out of their hopeless weakness. And one father gave a clear answer: the salvation that Christianity speaks of is different; for Christian salvation is not just a question of relying on God—in addition the believer must retain with all his might a strength of heart. But it is precisely in this point that the teaching has slowly been twisted and changed in this swamp called Japan.[45]

A second motivating force Christianity's dialogue with Buddhism is "the desire to build a bridge to Buddhism, among which Japanese Christianity is living as a tiny minority." Van Bragt calls this the "dialogical motive." Dialogue here is a way to communicate meaningfully with non-Christians in Japan and to do so as a matter of necessity. As the Japanese Catholic theologian Honda Masaaki has remarked, "the theological effort to reformulate the Christian faith with the help of Buddhist logic is today... an inescapable providential task for us, Japanese Christian scholars."[46]

Van Bragt's third stimulus for engaging Japanese Buddhism in dialogue is "a liberation motive." By this he means the theological attempt "to *replace* the Greek categories with the more intrinsically religious categories of Buddhism, and with the help endeavor to elaborate a theology that is truer to the Gospel message."[47] To understand Christian teachings on salvation, God, and the world, Japanese Christians find Buddhist modes of thought more understandable than Greek philosophy. Needless to say, the "liberating" aim of the dialogue is not to appropriate Buddhism as a kind of *ancilla theologiae* but to radically challenge theological presuppositions long considered self-evident. A good example is the attempt of Keel Hee Sung, a Korean theologian and scholar of religion, to interpret Jesus through the Buddhist concept of bodhisattva. Instead of the *Logos*-Christology that came to birth in the soil of Greek philosophy, Keel argues that a *bodhisattva*-Christology would appeal more directory to the spirituality of Asian peoples. The following statement is a direct reflection of Van Bragt's call to replace Greek categories with the vernacular categories of Buddhism."

> Now Asian Christians can respond to the question, "Who do you say that I am?," "You are the one who revealed to us most concretely and powerfully the image of a bodhisattva that has captivated our hearts." In their turn, Buddhists reserve every right to call Jesus simply one of the innumerable bodhisattvas, and Jesus is ultimately the same. But for the Christians who have traditionally rejected the docetic view of Jesus—and hence may not be satisfied with the docetic tendency in the Mahāyāna conception of the bodhisattva—Jesus is the person who realized concretely and decisively the ideal of the power that makes all bodhisattva bodhisattvas, that is, the power of love and Emptiness.[48]

Keel stands firm in the conviction that truth, including religious truth, is always historically mediated. At the same time, his view of history remains grounded in the incarnation of the Logos, that is, in the process of the truth's coming to realization like a line with a single starting point or a circle with a single center. For Christianity, the point of departure is always belief in Jesus as the Christ. Across all cultural and historical contexts, Jesus remains the subject of faith and can never be reduced to a predicate describing something else.

Keel's position opens itself to further development without compromising his initial aims. To think of Jesus as one bodhisattva among many is more than just one more Christological assertion. The image of Jesus Bodhisattva overturns received notions of Jesus as the absolute subject of faith and the starting point of history.[49] To view Jesus as a bodhisattva dislodges him from the center of history. That much is already implied in the idea of a bodhisattva as a selfless being without a substance of its own, never a unique subject capable of monopolizing the faith of others. To confess Jesus Bodhisattva is to transform the Christian view of reality, to deconstruct the notion of a starting point of history and with it the notions of, substance, subject, and eventually faith itself. To believe in Jesus as a bodhisattva is to be liberated from the demand that faith be grounded in one absolute, irreplaceable moment in history. Faith is only faith when it is free of all attachments, including the attachment to the idea of history as the realization of a single truth.

Viewed this way, Jesus Bodhisattva offers us the kind of theological conversion (*Kehre*) we have been pursuing, namely the shift from seeing Buddhism as an object for theology to accepting Buddhist thinking as part of the subjective framework from which we do theology. Buddhism is an essential element in the subjectivity of Christian faith in Asia. It is not an objective (exterior) "other *without*" but a subjective (interior) "other *within*." The Buddhist tradition does not run parallel to the Christian in Asia. The two are entangled at the roots. Almost without exception, scholarly attempts to relate Christian faith to the spirituality of other religious traditions do so on the assumption that, both historically and theologically, these traditions stand outside Christianity, when, in fact, they are the "other" within. Only a thorough revision of the theological framework in Asia can hope to turn this around.

In this connection, I would mention the work of Pyun Sun Hwan (1927–1995),[50] a Korean thinker who played a substantial role in bringing interreligious dialogue and religious pluralism to bear on Christian theology. Pyun advocated for a paradigm shift in approach from "theology *and* other religions" to "theology *through* other religions." In this way, the so-called "other religions" of Asia would form an integral part of the subjectivity of those who engage in theology. In his conclusion to a 1985 essay on "Other Religions and Theology," composed in commemoration of the one hundredth anniversary of the Christian mission in Korea, Pyun summarized his call for a new theological framework:

> The theme initially assigned to me was "other religions and theology." It goes without saying, to think of theology in connection with other religions, we need first to stop accusing other religions and to overcome our religious imperialism and its exclusivism. We also need to rescind the inclusivist tendency to regard other religions as a form of *preparatio evangelica*. In a religiously pluralized world, the theological zeal for converting people to Christianity no longer has a place. An honest dialogue with other religions is what is called for.... Other religions are not, as Western theology assumes, mere tools for doing theology. They are its very purpose. Other religions are not mere objects of theology. They belongs to its very subjectivity. I therefore propose that the right theme for us is not "theology *and* other religions," but "theology *through* other religions."[51]

For Pyun, the task facing Christian theology in Asia begins with abandoning the monologue for dialogue. As someone deeply engaged in interreligious dialogue with Buddhism, he was well aware of the limits of indigenous theology. As long as Christianity continued to use the traditional religions of Asia merely as a tool for the effective transmission of its own faith, it would continue to objectify them. Pyun's idea of doing theology *through* other religions brings that problem into clear relief.

But how can Christianity treat the other religions in its surroundings without objectifying them? What are Christians to expect from the encounter with the "other within"? In Chapters 4 and 5 we will take up this idea of doing theology through an appropriation of other faiths and its challenge to Christianity's established idea of reality as monocentric.

THE PLACE OF HUMAN BEINGS IN NATURE

Natural science and the decentering process

The impact of the rise of the natural sciences on our idea of the human is aptly captured in Sigmund Freud's claim that humanity was made to experience "from the hand of science two great outrages upon its naive self-love."[52] With the scientific discoveries associated with the names of Copernicus and Darwin, human beings were unwillingly displaced from places they had once regarded as their own. As Freud said, they were "no longer masters in their own homes." The Copernican revolution dislodged the human race from the "center" of the universe; the Darwinian revolution followed by taking away its "peculiar privilege" among all living things. As we remarked in the previous chapter, of all the sciences, it was biology that raised the most radical questions to the way human beings understood themselves and their world.

Pierre Baldi, a specialist in bioinformatics, observed that "the history of Western science and civilization has been a history of the progress of decentering, a gradual movement away from a self-centered view of the world that comes so naturally to us."[53] The seventeenth century had brought about a paradigm shift from a geocentric universe to a heliocentric one. Like a great display of fireworks, it signaled the decentering of the human in the cosmos. In the nineteenth century, the Darwinian revolution invalidated worldviews based on a *scala naturae* that guaranteed human beings a secure position between the divine and animal spheres. Slowly, they had to adjust to seeing themselves as adrift in a wild natural world, which was itself adrift in a vast cosmos. These two revolutions came to a crescendo in the manipulation of DNA, the elementary units of information that are thought to distinguish one human being from another human being and all human beings from other living things. Research soon made it clear that all living things share large parts of their DNA. The boundaries between the human and the non-human that had survived the two great revolutions continued to fade, and with it, humanity's hope of retaining a central place in reality.

While all of this was unfolding at the macrocosmic level, changes were also underway on the microcosmic level with regard to self-consciousness of our bodies and our sexuality. Baldi goes so far as to suggest the emergence of a new form of humanity—the "posthuman"—based on a succession of three breakthroughs in human sexuality: the birth of a test-tube baby by IVF (in vitro fertilization), human cloning, and DNA manipulation. He draws particular attention to human cloning for its impact on our self-understanding.[54] Behind each of these advances stands a view of humans as computer-like "biological information-process machines."[55]

The birth of Dolly, the cloned sheep, marked a watershed in the arrival of that new way of looking at human beings. It also shocked us into the realization that if we, like the sheep, are mammals, then we, too, could be cloned. It was no longer a question of what was theoretically possible but of what was practically within reach. It raised the fundamental question of who we are and what it is that makes us human beings. In any case, the debate over nature vs. nurture would seem to safeguard us against DNA or gene-based determinism. As long as a clone and its original are two different persons, at least theoretically, that would seem to leave the notion of the self unscathed. But matters are not so simple, as Baldi's questions remind us:

> Studies of identical twins have shown over and over a degree of similarity that goes beyond the physical, and includes many traits, habits, and behaviors. And think how you would feel if you were sitting in a room with ten clones of yourself? Would it not be a little unsettling? And what about living in a town with 1 million clones of yourself? Such events have essentially zero probability of occurring under natural conditions, but become a simple matter of resources once the technology is available.[56]

Cloning a person's identical twin obliges us to clarify "whether and when we ought to say that two organisms, and in particular two human beings, are identical."[57] It shakes us out of the "evolutionary illusion" of refusing to see the "underlying continuity" between us and other living things. As Baldi argues, the only borderlines are those established by habit to distinguish one entity from the other:

> Through millions of years of evolution, our brains have been wired to provide us with an inner feeling of self, a feeling that each of us is a unique individual delimited by precise boundaries.... A fundamental argument of the book is that this self-centered view of the world is problematic—in fact, it is "scientifically" wrong. It is the result of evolutionary accidents. The reason for its past success lies in being an adequate model of the world during our evolutionary bootstrapping.... As we shall see, genome, computation, and minds are rather fluid and continuous entities, both in space and in time. Individually, we are just samples of this continuum. Myriad other selves are arbitrarily close to ours, selves continuously interpolated between ourselves and any other being, including those of the opposite sex.... The boundary between the self and the other, the self and the world, the inside and outside has begun to blur, and ultimately may evaporate entirely.[58]

As radical as Baldi's conclusions are, they remind us that all natural science affects our understanding of the human being and its place in the world. As humanity lost its place of privilege at the center of reality through the advance of modern science, it was inevitable that our idea of self-consciousness would be deconstructed. The decentering of the human being in science led to a sense that human awareness had also lost its center. The cry of Nietzsche's "madman" spoke to the anxiety of a modern consciousness that found itself without an ontological center on which to rely in a dynamic, evolving universe. The trauma is not only branded into our souls; it is to all appearances incurable. But if the demythifying effects of science have disenchanted us of our evolutionary illusions and exposed our credence to a "fictitious center of the world," they also suggest an over-reliance on "too naive a theology."[59] In this sense, Karl Rahner's claim that "directly or indirectly, all natural sciences involve anthropology"[60] is aimed squarely at the theologian. What science has to say about our identity and integrity as human individuals, positive or negative as the case may be, cannot be disposed of without betraying the theological vocation.

Science used by and for philosophy

Biology, as we have been saying, is critical for our discussion. Max Scheler's "philosophical anthropology" offers a valuable model for dealing with the questions natural science has posed to traditional images of the human. He is of one mind with Rahner's insistence that natural science influences our identity and integrity as human being in the way we understand ourselves. His pioneering attempts to reconstruct traditional anthropology by correlating human nature to scientific discovery reflected the general tendency in modern anthropology to describe the uniqueness of the human without recourse to the categories of the Christian faith, but only "through reflection on the place of humanity in nature and specifically through a comparison of human existence with that of the higher animals."[61]

In the same way that Troeltsch sought to interpret divine revelation through the historical method, Scheler sought an appreciation of the human beings through the methods of the natural sciences. In essence, they were branches of the same tree. Scheler's way of questioning the "special place" of the human being in nature marked a departure from the prescientific modes of thought he had inherited from Western intellectual history. Along with Helmut Plessner and Arnold Gehlen, he was convinced that natural science, and in particular, biology, were critical to the discussion. Thus, even as theology was turning itself in the direction of anthropology, Scheler was turning anthropology in the direction of science.

The revolution in philosophical anthropology prompted by the growing influence of scientific modes of thought affected the human sciences in general. As we noted the Darwinian revolution and its consequence from the biological sciences brought the meaning value of religion, Christianity included, into question. Scheler's philosophy was a response to this "outrage." Insofar as Scheler sought to reinterpret traditional religious and philosophical anthropology in the light of natural science, he paralleled Troeltsch, whose aim was to reinterpret Christianity's claim to absoluteness by employing the methods of historicism. From a broader perspective, we might say that Scheler represented a preparatory stage in a scientific study of religion, which would later develop into the cognitive science of religion.

Modern anthropology takes it as a matter of course that the physical makeup of human beings is described in comparison with that of animals. Scheler's concern with a philosophy of human nature fully integrated with natural science can be already in his 1926 lecture "Human Beings and History":

> If there is an philosophical task facing our age that presses on us for a solution, it is that of a philosophical anthropology. What I mean by that is a fundamental science of the *being* and *esential structure* of human being; of its relationship to the realms of nature (inorganic, plant, and animal) that ground it to all things; of its metaphysical origins as well as of its physical, mental, and spiritual beginning in the world; of the forces and power that move humans and that they themselves control; of the basic orientation and laws that govern its biological, psychological, intellectual, and social development with regard to both its essential potential and its actuality. Only such an anthropology is capable of being applies to all sciences that have as their object "the human."[62]

Scheler's ambition was for an anthropological synthesis of range of disciplines including medicine, archeology, ethnology, history, sociology, psychology, and above all, the natural sciences. He was open to scientific perspectives on human beings without predetermined limits. We see this reiterated in his 1928 book *The Human Place in the Cosmos*, in which he set out explicitly to investigate the "essence of human being in relation to plants and animals" in hope of arriving its "special place in the cosmos" in a metaphysical sense. He saw his task as a serious challenge never before encountered in human history, one that drove him to pursue a "common foundation"[63] to the anthropological worldviews of the Judeo-Christian tradition, the ancient Greek tradition, and the natural sciences in the broad sense of the term.

The very fact that Scheler should concentrate on a "common foundation" is an indication of how seriously traditional views of human being had been shaken and dismantled by natural science. Scheler recognized better than many that Darwin's research into the origins of species reduced humans to a stage of evolutionary development, differentiating them from other living things only "by degrees of complexity of the energies and abilities inherited from ancestors in the animal world and found in subhuman nature."[64] His anxiety was not only for the effect this had on traditional anthropology but also for the incompetence of science to solve the questions it was raising. Indeed, for Scheler, the harder science tried to uncover the unique nature of human being, the more it obscured its special place in nature.

As Scheler saw it, the most rational way to a common foundation from which theology, philosophy, and science can study the human was to abandon received views and to rebuild our view of human beings from the ground up, free of assumptions or other methodological deflections. In all of this, Scheler's similarities to Troeltsch are in evidence, as is the honesty with which he recognized the power traditional ideas have over us. Accordingly, his aim was to respect the *content* of the idea of human being inherited from the past without having to accept its *explanation*—like transferring old wine to new wineskins. He begins his argument by noting the biological definition of the "human being"

> as a subclass of vertebrates and mammals; no matter what the consequences of this may be, it is quite clear that the human being is here not only *subordinated* to the concept of "animal" but also occupies a very small corner of the animal realm.[65]

The conventional idea of human being, in contrast, is "essentialist." Scheler's aim, accordingly is to examine "whether or not this essential concept, which links humans to a special place that is not comparable to any other special place any other species may have, is a justified concept."[66]

To understand the unique characteristics of a human being in comparison with other living things such as plants and animals, Scheler proposed up a process by which the "bio-psychic structure"[67] of life unfolds in four stages. The animate being's relationship to itself and its surroundings begins from a first, rudimentary stage of "impulsion." At this point it lacks the functions of consciousness, sensation, and representation but is capable of growth and reproduction. At the second stage, "instinct," the animate being shows purposive action for itself and other living beings, such as nutrition and care of its young. For behavior to qualify as instinctive, it must be repeated in fixed patterns and transmitted congenitally to the next generation. The third stage, "associative memory," is exhibited in previous behavior being *slowly but steadily modified.*"[68] Pavlov's experiments with "conditioned reflex" laid bare the nature and mechanism of associate memory at work. It is attained and then passed on as "tradition" to offspring through learning and imitation. Animals living in social groups display this level of development, only human beings can step free of tradition, relativize its power over them, and negate or transform it by the exercise of reason. This fourth and highest stage, "practical intelligence," allows us to solve the problems and adapt to new circumstances. Experiments show that human beings share this function with other primates, such as chimpanzees.

Scheler recognized that his bio-psychic model was not sufficient to clarify the difference between human beings and higher animals. He rejected the idea that the answer lay in the presence or absence of intelligence, or even in degrees of intelligence. He insisted that there must be an essential, qualitative difference to the human intellect—an "x-principle," of which he remarks, "The new principle is, first of all, *opposite anything we call life, including life in the human being*: it is a genuinely new, essential fact which cannot at all be reduced to the 'natural evolution of life.'"[69] This factor, to which Scheler attributes the unique status of the human being among all other living things, the animate world, he names "spirit." It lifts the human beings out of the dependencies and necessities of ordinary animate life:

The ultimate determination of a being with spirit—no matter what its psycho-physical makeup—is its existential detachment from organic being, its freedom and detachability—and the detachment of its center of existence from the bondage to, the pressure of, and the organic dependence on "life" and everything which belongs to life, and thus also its detachment from its own drive-related "intelligence."[70]

Hence, a being with spirit is not bound to its instincts and surrounding environment. If anything, it is "non-environmental," in the sense that it is capable of transcending its surroundings. Its world is always a "world opening out."[71]

What, then, is the origin of this spirit? Scheler was not satisfied with "negative theory" that attributed spiritual freedom from the environment to organ deficiency. Paul Alsberg, a representative of this view, argued that "spirit" is a name for the lack of instinctive bonds that keep living things bound to their surrounding. For Scheler, this amounted to the claim "spirit is only a late surrogate for a lack of organic adaptation,"[72] and was incapable of answering the crucial question regarding the special place of human beings in the natural world:

> On what different foundation do the sublimated drives produce neurosis in one case, and cultural activity on the other? Which way does sublimation go? Why do the principles of spirit (at least in part) coincide with the principles of Being? And finally: what is the purpose of sublimation, of repression, of negating the will to life-and for the sake of what ultimate values and purposes is all this happening?[73]

At this point, Scheler revealed his loyalty to the traditional viewpoint of human uniqueness and broke camp with scientific and materialistic explanations. The human spirit that distinguishes us metaphysically from other life forms, could not be attributed to the absence of natural instinct. Only the presence of something more can account for the fact that "the human place in the cosmos is outside the cosmos":

> Any form of the negative theories presupposes what it wants to explain: spirit and reason, an indigenous lawfulness of spirit as well as a partial identity of spirit's principles with those of Being. It is spirit that initiates the repression of drives in that the spiritual will, guided by ideas and values, rejects the impulses of our drive-life that counter the [positive] ideas and values and the necessary images [*Vorstellungen*] of drive-driven actions. And, on the other hand, it lures the lurking drives with the bait of appropriate images of ideas and values to

coordinate drive impulses so that they will execute the project of the will, posited by spirit, and make it real.[74]

Once again, Scheler finds it necessary to revert to the Christian metaphysical tradition that sees human beings as possessed of an immortal soul. In seeking meaning to the world and teaching beyond for what transcends this world, we exercise our ability to keep a distance from the world, and confirms the reality of a human spirit whose rightful place is ultimately outside the cosmos.

In a word, Scheler's anthropology stood midway between the traditional Christianity and modern science. He selected only those elements from the scientific view of human beings that coincided with his fidelity to tradition. The double standard to which the notion of "spirit" drove him beyond the boundaries of science. Here again, like Troeltsch, who had tried to unite historicism and mysticism, Scheler was forced to loosen his grip on the methods of natural science in order to main a firm grip on the transcendental foundations of the human.

THE SCIENTIFIC EXPLANATION OF RELIGION

The reality of the human spirit frustrated Scheler's initial goal of locating the uniqueness of human beings scientifically. He concluded that, on this matter, science could best serve philosophy by acknowledging its limits. Philosophical anthropology after Scheler took a different direction from the foundations he had tried to lay. The "negative theory" he had so roundly rejected was taken up again by Arnold Gehlen in his concept of "deficient beings" (*Mangelwesen*). Gehlen was more committed to the scientific method and its explanations than Scheler had been and saw no reason to revert to timeworn notions of "spirit" to identify the uniqueness of human beings. Insofar as human beings are able to stand free of their environmental conditions, this is not due to a nonmaterial force beyond the reach of science, but could be explained by a deprivation of those instincts that bind animate beings mechanically to their surroundings. This apparent inferiority to other animals also accounts for human superiority in observing, remembering, and modifying the world about them:

If, in comparison to animals, man appears as a "deficient being," then this designation expresses a comparative relationship and is therefore of limited value and not a concept of real substance. In this respect, this concept attempts precisely what H. Freyer criticizes it for: "One envisions man fictitiously as animal only to discover that he makes an imperfect and indeed impossible animal." The designation "deficient being" is intended to convey the following: From a biological point of view, in comparison to animals, the structure of the human body appears to be a paradox and stands out sharply. This designation does not, of course, completely define man but it does serve to point out his special position from a morphological perspective.[75]

The deficiency of instinct that gave birth to culture was reason enough to account for the unique *place* of human beings in the natural world. There was no need to follow Scheler in appealing unscientific, metaphysical concepts.

Gehlen typifies natural science's refusal to play a role in support of traditional notions of what it means to be human. Quite the opposite, scientific methods and research have slowly but resolutely been eroding the metaphysical and theological ground on which those notions have rested for centuries. For the natural sciences the goal of reducing all religious phenomena without remainder to scientific principles is no longer a matter for dispute. When the sociobiologist Edward O. Wilson proposed a "consilience" of all academic disciplines, he did so on the assumption that the trend toward scientific explanations of religion was already irreversible. What he means by *consilience* is a "jumping together of knowledge by the linking of facts and fact-based theory across disciplines to create a common groundwork of explanation."[76] In effect, it aims at a synthesis, based on sociobiological principles, of everything known about human beings and other living things.

Naturally, Wilson includes religious phenomena in the synthesis. However complex religion may be, eventually it is open to being "mapped onto the two dimensions of genetic advantage and evolutionary change."[77] Religions have survived because they have helped their adherents survive in the face of competing environmental forces. The cognition and behavior of human beings, the basis of all human culture, is ultimately regulated by what Wilson calls "epigenetic rules":

> Culture is created by the communal mind, and each mind in turn is the product of the genetically structured human brain. Genes and culture are therefore

inseverably linked. But the linkage is flexible, to a degree still mostly unmeasured. The linkage is also tortuous: Genes prescribe epigenetic rules, which are the neural pathways and regularities in mental development by which the individual mind assembles itself. The mind grows from birth to death by absorbing parts of the existing culture available to it, with selections guided by the epigenetic rules inherited by the individual brain.[78]

Seen from this perspective, religion and morality foreit all transcendental privilege as fundamental cognitive and behavioral value systems. They are simply *a posteriori* effects of physiological processes. Scientific research in sociobiology, neuroscience, the cognitive science of religion, and the like, each in is own way arrives at the same conclusion: religions and ethics, long considered the quintessential elements in human self-understanding, can be explained as nothing more and nothing less than relics of the natural evolution of the human race.

As we see from the title of his book, *Religion as a Natural Phenomenon,* makes plain, Daniel Dennett is a strong advocate of this position:

> Like other animals, we have built-in desires to reproduce and to do pretty much whatever it takes to achieve this goal, but we also have creeds, and the ability to transcend our genetic imperatives. This fact does make us different, but it is itself a biological fact, visible to natural science, and something that requires an explanation from natural science.[79]

When Dennet insists that religion is a "natural" phenomenon, he does not mean to put it on a par with biological species and material things. He only wishes to insist that its origins are not "supernatural," that "it is a human phenomenon composed of events, organisms, objects, structures, patterns, and the like that all obey the laws of physics or biology, and hence do not involve miracles."[80] To approach religious phenomena in a purely scientific manner, Dennett warns that we need to be released from the spell that religion casts on us and break "the taboo against a forthright, scientific, no-holds-barred investigation of religion as one natural phenomenon among many."[81] In this regard, his approach differs markedly from the more aggressive posture of the "new atheism" represented by Richard Dawkins and his thesis of "the God delusion." Dennett take a more cautious, agnostic view regarding the existence of spiritual reality, acknowledging that "it could be true that God exists, that God is indeed the intelligent, conscious, loving creator of us all." Nevertheless, so long as concepts like "God" belong to the complex reality we call religion, it, too, is "a perfectly natural phenomenon."

To prove that religion qualifies as a purely natural phenomenon, Dennett draws on research that explains the emergence and transmission of religious beliefs as part of the general evolution of the human mind. In particular, the cognitive science of religion on how the mind represents and acquires religious ideas, and what the practical consequences of these ideas are in human behavior. If religion can be understood adequately by "our ordinary, natural cognitive resources"[82] and without recourse to the methods of theology and philosophy, we may conclude that religion is not an extraordinary phenomenon at all. Thus, the cognitive approach to religion weighs on Christianity to acknowledge that all religious phenomena, including belief in the existence of a spiritual realm and a divine being, are by-products of natural evolution.

Theoretical research into the cognitive science of religion intensified in the 1970s and has flourished into the twenty-first century with a steady stream of publications and the foundation of the International Association for the Cognitive Science of Religion (IACSR) in 2006. Recent discussions on the evolutionary dimensions of the question have broadened out to demonstrate commonalities in the development of distincitively religions patterns of thought and behavior across social and cultural boundaries. In this vein, Stewart Gutherie points to the fundamental human tendency to interpret ambiguous though completely natural phenomena to a specific agent:

> If the wind buffets one's front door, for example, one first thinks that it may be a visitor. A runner in the park wishes to know whether an upright shape glimpsed near his path is that of another human, or merely of a drinking fountain, a shrub, or a pile of trash bags against a tree, or whether a sound behind him is running human footsteps or blowing leaves, and if human whether it is merely an echo of himself. Although a human-like model subsequently may be discarded if another model clearly is better, it usually is tried before others.[83]

It is not unreasonable to assume that this cognitive ability would work in favor of human beings struggling to survive within and adapt to natural surroundings filled with dangerous predators. Anthropomorphism, a common feature in religious traditions, ascribes human-like forces at work in the environment that might not actually exist. Justin Barret takes this idea of Guthrie's a step further to argue that religion can be explained as a "hyperactive agent-detection device":

> Thus, people are particularly sensitive to the presence of intentional agency and seem biased to overattribute intentional action as the cause of a given state of affairs when data is ambiguous or sketchy. These observations suggest that whatever cognitive mechanism people have for detecting agency might be extremely sensitive; in other words, people can be said to possess hyperactive agent-detection devices (HADD). According to Guthrie, such a biased perceptual device would have been quite adaptive in our evolutionary past, for the consequences of failing to detect an agent are potentially much graver than mistakenly detecting an agent that is not there.[84]

Pascal Boyer, a leading figure in the field, clarifies that it is the very "counterintuitive" character of imaginary agency that makes it more likely to receive attention and be transmitted to the next generation:

> Religious believers and skeptics generally agree that religion is a dramatic phenomenon that requires a dramatic explanation, either as a spectacular revelation of truth or as a fundamental error of reasoning. Cognitive science and neuroscience suggest a less dramatic but perhaps more empirically grounded picture of religion as a probable, although by no means inevitable by-products of the normal operation of human cognition.[85]

Boyer engages in what we may call the "biocultural study of religion," an approach that aims to

> support the claim that supernatural agent conceptions are naturally reproduced in human thought as a result of evolved *cognitive* mechanisms that hyperactively detect agency when confronted with ambiguous phenomena and, once conceived, is culturally nurtured as a result of evolved coalitional mechanisms that hyperactively protect in-group cohesion.[86]

Boyer argues that all forms of religion originate from cognitive systems in the brain that allow us to experience and recognize the world. Among the many and varied religious concepts human cognition has come up with, those that have survived are the "relatively successful ones."[87] Boyer's focus is to demonstrate how religion comes to emerge in the process of selection, given that at all times and all the time, indefinitely many variants of religious notions were and are created inside individual minds. Not all these variants are equally successful in cultural transmission. What we call a cultural phenomenon is the result of a selection that is taking place all the time and everywhere.[88]

This means that the religious idea that are still with us represents only a small portion of the multitude of ideas that have passed through the mind over time. Some of them, Boyer observes, were abandoned in the selection process because they impeded adaptation to the natural world. Following E. O. Wilson, R. Boyd, P. Richerson, W. Durham, and others, he also balances the role of genetic inheritance with that of cultural transmission. (We recall here that Dawkins coined the term "meme" to describe a cultural transmitter parallel to the "gene" as genetic transmitter.)

In the attempt to explain how religious concepts like God and spirit emerge, Boyer suggests we look on the human mind as a set of templates that can be adjusted to process new information. As long as our perception of the world agrees with our expectations, we rely on a kind of "intuitive ontology." But when those expectations are violated, religious representations emerge to restore the balance. Religious images and ideas have a "mnemonic advantage" when it comes to what is transmitted to succeeding generations, which explains their privileged position vis-à-vis other modes of thought. To take an analogy, the front view of a tiger's face leaves a stronger impression on memory than a side view because staring a tiger in the face demands an immediate decision to fight or flee. That memory is privileged precisely because it is more important for survival, which is also why it is selected for passing down to the next generation.

This same function of mnemonic templates can be extended to include phenomena that are not directly experienced. Boyer argues that we may find "catalogs of supernatural templates"[89] governing religious concepts that violate the "intuitive expectations" resulting from our "default inferences" about the way things work in the world. For example, our intuition leads us to assume that no person can see everything in the world at once. Accordingly, the notion of a personal being who sees and knows everything is a "salient cognitive artifact"[90] that violates our intuitive expectations. The ability to imagine a supernatural person who, even though invisible to us, sees the whole world and who exists everywhere at the same time, suggests a "human capacity for decoupling representations."[91] The concept of an omniscient and omnipresent transcendental being like God would then be the by-product of the cognitive function of the brain for creating "hypothetical scenarios" that allow us to imagine how what we see might look like to someone else from another standpoint. A "supernatural" concept is more useful for survival in the face of danger because it activates the "agency-detection system" that functions as a "predator-avoidance-system" and "prey-detection-system":

> This is in fact the way people represent ancestors and gods the world over. People experience particular situations. Some information about these situations is strategic, that is, activates their inference systems for social interaction (cheating, trust evaluation, gossip, social exchange, coalition building, etc.). They also represent that there are supernatural agents around. Now they spontaneously assume that these agents have access to all the strategic information about that particular situation, even though they themselves may not have access to all of it.[92]

Boyer has this to say regarding the importance of "decoupling" for securing survival:

> Decoupled cognition is crucial to human cognition because we depend so much on information communicated by others and on cooperation with others. To evaluate information provided by others you must build some mental simulation of what they describe. Also, we could not carry out complex hunting expeditions, tool making, food gathering or social exchange without complex planning....
>
> Decoupled cognition appears very early in children's development when they start to "pretend-play," using a variety of objects as though they were other objects (e.g., a bar of soap as a car, a puppet as a person, etc.).... Decoupling is also necessary to produce external representations, another universal capacity in humans. Toys, statues, rock paintings and finger drawings in the sand are not the same as what they represent. To make sense of them, our inference systems must block certain inferences—the path through the forest is one inch wide on the drawing but it is not that narrow in actual fact—and maintain others—that the path in the sand turns left means that the actual one turns left too. So the interpretation of external representations can be subtle. Indeed, in many cases we intuitively consider that what external representations stand for depends much more on their creators' intentions than on what they look like.[93]

As such, religious concepts are a combination of "ontological labels" and "counterintuitive tags." To survive in nature, human beings need as much information as possible, even when that information runs counter to intuitive expectations. Belief in the ability to communicate with an omnipotent and omniscient being through a shaman or some other mediator has helped human beings survive. The ideas of God and spirit as "special persons" serve as counterintuitive points of referral insofar as they are endowed with "strategic information"[94] for safeguarding human beings against the perils of existence in a hostile environment. In a word, religious beliefs are by-products of natural evolution, inventions of the mind that direct human beings to behave in accord with their native instinct for survival. The spiritual realm in its entirety can therefore be reduced to cognitive functions of the brain.

Troeltsch's theological goal of enlisting the support of other religions to explain the incontestable absoluteness of Christianity was doomed from the start by the rise of the science of religion and the reality of multiple religious belonging. Similarly, Scheler's dream of enlisting the support of the natural sciences to reconfirm the traditional understanding of human uniqueness has been frustrated by advances in cognitive science that seek to reduce all religious ideas and behavior to evolutionary developments in the brain.

3

Dwelling in the Negative

As we saw in the cases of Troeltsch and Scheler, the *place* of privilege that Christian faith and philosophies based on it enjoyed in the intellectual history of the West was severely shaken and finally overcome by the scientific method. Theology has had to face the inconvenient fact that the study of *history* has relativizes the absoluteness of the Christian faith, and that the study of *nature* has threatened to uproot religions from their transcendental grounding. That more and more theologians should feel themselves driven into a *cul-de-sac* and fearing extinction is hardly to be wondered at.

But *what kind of Christianity* is it that theology considers threatened by the study of religion and the methods of science? If religion and science are joining forces to proclaim the end of Christianity, *what kind of end* is it? On the answers to those questions hangs the future of the transmission of the faith.

FINIS CHRISTIANISMI REDUX REVERSED

Let us begin by recalling the theological declaration of the end of Christianity, *finis christianismi*, issued by the Swiss theologian Franz Overbeck (1837–1905). Viewing our present-day theological crisis through the lens of Overbeck's diagnosis can help us identify the roots of the issue.

What forced this "quiet, bookish mien of the archetypical scholar"[1] to utter such harsh words about the end of Christianity? Could it be that the challenge of the *finis christianismi* has returned today in the form of the deconstructive critiques of religion and science? If so, does that mean we are to endorse Overbeck's declaration for our own times? In the concluding paragraph of his monumental survey of the revolution in nineteenth-century thought, Karl Löwith suggests just that:

> Whoever will take the trouble to pursue Overbeck's train of thought will perceive in the labyrinth of his sentences, so full of reservations, the straight and daring of an absolutely honest mind. He elucidated the problem which Christianity presents for us. In the typical figures of the nineteenth century, he made clear the abyss separating us from Christianity. Since Hegel, and particularly through the work of Marx and Kierkegaard, the Christianity of this bourgeois-Christian world has come to an end. This does not mean that a faith which once conquered the world perishes with its last secular manifestations. For how should the Christian pilgrimage *in hoc saeculo* ever become homeless (*heimatlos*) in the land where it has never been at home?[2]

When Overbeck set out at the beginning of the last century to ask how Christian theology at the time, he made it clear that he "would not be concerned with anything other than proving the *finis christianismi* in modern Christianity."[3] Like Friedrich Nietzsche, his colleague in the faculty of philosophy, Overbeck was an "untimely" (*unzeitgemäss*) thinker. People referred to the two of them as an "alliance in arms" (*Waffengenossenschaft*).[4] Overbeck's declaration of the end of Christianity and Nietzsche's proclamation of the death of God echoed off one another. Nietzsche dedicated the first part of his *Untimely Meditations* to Overbeck in 1873, the same year that Overbeck published his controversial work *On the Christian Nature of Theology Today*.

Overbeck had received his theological training at the University of Göttingen, the center of the "history of religions" school represented by such thinkers as Herman Gunkel, Johannes Weiss, and Wilhelm Bousset. These biblical theologians focused their research on how religious texts reflect the mutual influence of religions in general, and in particular, how early Christian texts were the product of Jewish and Greek culture. Their historical-critical investigations led them to conclude that the eschatological faith of the early Christians differed sharply from the way it was received in succeeding generations. This was the basis for Overbeck's claim that the expectation of an imminent *parousia Christi* among the early Christians was extinguished and replaced by absorption of faith into secular history. By releasing the faith from the expectation of a second coming, Christianity realigned itself with secular philosophical wisdom, which marked the beginnings of Christian theology. For Overbeck, the entire history of Christianity was a gradual process of the concealment and decay (*Abfall*) of the faith through ongoing compromise with secular history and culture. Rejecting Hegel's view of history as reconciliation, Overbeck saw it as nothing other than an "abyss in which Christianity has been catapulted against its will."[5] As Löwith notes, his "basic distinction between the history of the 'origins' of Christianity and the history of its 'decay' stands firmly against the progressive and optimistic schema Hegel had devised."[6] As a result,

> theology makes Christianity as a religion problematic. In other words, it calls its whole status as a religion into question... Even apologetic theology, were it to have proved rationally that Christianity were true would have destroyed it as a as a religion.[7]

Albrecht Ritschl, Adolf von Harnack, Ernst Troeltsch, and others associated with the liberal Protestant theology (*Kulturprotestantismus*) current at the time had sought to understand Christianity as a historical phenomenon. For Overbeck, the whole project was contradicted by its transhistorical aim of extracting the essence of Christianity from "the primordially Christian" (*das Urchristliche*). His interest in monasticism, Franciscan spirituality, and pietism are indicative of how he himself understood the Christian faith. Anxiety over the impending end of the world that had colored the faith of the early Christians receded and marked a *finis christianismi* without a new order having been ushered in to replace the old.[8] Through the forfeiture of its otherworldly character to secular modes of thought, a gap opened in Christianity between faith and theology that could only distort and spoil its essence. Overbeck invited modern theology to acknowledge that very abyss at its own feet:

> My view was: It can't go on like this! If theology continues to chatter like this, Xsthm [Christenthum] will soon be chattered to death. So how are things going on now? Theology has became chattier than ever.... But is this really so different from a Xsthm that has been chattered to death?[9]

Christian theology did away with an otherworldly faith that fundamentally negates the secular world. This ascetic, world-renouncing character of the faith exhibits a distinctive "wisdom of death" whose original spirit was preserved in the monastic life which had inherited the early Christian ideal of martyrdom as a martyrdom of the everyday (*martyrium quotidiamum*).

It is unclear if Overbeck ever intended to construct his own theology out of the rubble of his radical critique. What is clear, as Löwith observed, is that

> Overbeck was fully aware that religious problems must be placed upon a completely new foundation, "even at the cost of what has up to now been called religion."... This will not happen until we humans recognize that we go forward only by losing our foothold from time to time; we live our lives under conditions which do not permit us to evade this experiment.... This loss of foothold Overbeck took as his own position between culture and Christianity.[10]

Löwith relates Overbeck's positive view of the "loss of foothold" to his admiration for Nietzsche's courage in facing problems. He goes on to cite Walter Nigg's appraisal of Overbeck:

> The unique and significant aspect of Overbeck's elucidation of the relationship between Christianity and culture is the fact that it does not give any solution. All solutions would come into conflict with his basic axiom. Overbeck's merit consists in having demonstrated the impossibility of any solution, at least of any solution which man as he is today could contrive by his own efforts.[11]

Somewhat paradoxically, Overbeck's anti-theological thinking influenced neoorthodox theologians like Karl Barth, who, like Overbeck, criticized the trend toward cultural Protestantism and promoted an idea of God as "the wholly other," *totaliter aliter*.[12] Barth considered Overbeck a frontier thinker willing to take a stand "at the outermost limits of the possibility of religion," and yet found his "sense of awe" (*Ehrfurcht*) "too risky and too dangerous for us."[13] It is also generally agreed that Heidegger's reading Overbeck in the early 1910s was a stimulus for the idea of "being-toward-death."[14] With Overbeck, he saw the radical expectation of the second coming of Christ among the early Christians as an example of the "authentic experience of life" (*die faktische Lebenserfahrung*) that leads us to question the meaning of our existence in the face of death.[15]

Despite Overbeck's insistence that the otherworldliness of the faith be rooted in this world, Löwith's question remains: how is it even possible that "the Christian pilgrimage *in hoc saeculo* ever become homeless in a land where it has never been at home?" The "homelessness" of Christianity is not achieved in a superhistorical state but in a radical historicity. In fact, Overbeck's thesis about the end of Christianity grew out of his historical approach to its origins. His enthusiasm for the history of religions was not that different from Troeltsch's eagerness to place Christianity among the other world religions.[16] For neither of them did this imply a secularization of the faith. Overbeck situated the essence of the faith in a realm far removed from human history, which can only be viewed *sub specie aeternitatis*. It is "a mystery, hidden in a darkness so profound that at best the historian can only discern general shapes within it," and that " primordial history"(*die Urges-chichte*) and "the primordially Christian" (*das Urchristliche*) have "nothing to do with the chronological pre-history of humanity."[17] Similarly, Troeltsch's adoption of the historical method led him to conclude that Christianity, along with all religious traditions, are all pathways to a transcendental divinity beyond history. For these two German theologians, as indispensable as history was for talk about God, they held fast to the belief that the essence and ground of faith lay beyond history.

Overbeck's declaration of the end of Christianity, then, was of a piece with his belief in its prehistorical and superhistorical nature. The situation is reversed today. It is no longer Christianity but religion and science that have declared the end of Christianity. Paradoxically, Christianity has come to experience its end and homelessness not by denying the radical historicity of its essence but by affirming it—the "homelessness *in hoc saeculo*" of which Löwith spoke. The very strangeness and eccentricity of the Christian message in the world is the mark of its radical historicity. Although theology is always *in* history, it can never feel at home, because it is never *of* history. Accordingly, every theological endeavor must begin from the awareness that no matter when or where it takes place, its circumstances mark the end of Christianity.

The sense of homelessness is experienced not only by those who transmit a religious tradition but also by those who inherit it. It is part and parcel of Christian hermeneutics insofar as understanding the tradition is the ground of the believer's faith and self-understanding. Chronologically, tradition is a thing of the past. But when it is appropriated into understanding in the here and now, it is contemporaneous with the believer. The reason is obvious.

Viewed merely as the product of a distant past, tradition is an object that has no relation to our lives. But if, as we mentioned in Chapter 1, understanding always entails a movement of transcendence, a moving beyond ourselves, then self-understanding necessarily contains an element of self-negation. It is not enough to recognize our own deficiencies of intellect; we need to open up to something beyond ourselves. In religious terms, this means seeing tradition not as something at our disposal (*verfügbar*) but as something that disposes of us.

In this way, Overbeck's emphasis on the experience of homelessness as a mark of true faith and a sign of theology's failure to grasp the otherworldly essence of Christianity is decisive both for self-understanding and for fidelity to the tradition. In our context, the problems that religion and science have raised for theology are experienced as homelessness in a different sense. They have destroyed the home our faith once provided and left us wandering aimlessly, without a clear idea of what it means to be an authentic self. The Christian tradition can regain its position only if those who remain within it are able to negate the inauthenticity in their own self-understanding, if they can accept the homelessness that religion and science have forced upon the tradition as an existential problem for themselves.

In a word, understanding the tradition means understanding the radical disconnect of our times from the tradition as received. In our discussion of the hermeneutical nature of theology, we noted the sense in which the experience of alienation from a religious tradition can be a condition for its genuine acceptance. Only when believers accept the historicity of their faith and realize that the *place* from which they seek to understand makes them *dead* to the tradition inherited from the past are they able to renew the tradition. In this sense, homelessness is more than religious vagrancy. It is a path to "authentic historicity," an occasion to show "anticipatory resoluteness" to "authentic existence."[18] Such was the case with Overbeck when he proclaimed the end of Christianity, and with Troeltsch when he claimed that the historical method had "shattered" Christianity's dogmatic modes of self-understanding. Both saw that the homelessness they felt in the theology of their times was in fact a permanent feature of all theology, whetever the particular hermeneutical conditions in which it happened to find itself struggling to inherit the Christian past.

The sense of homelessness that religion and science bring to theology today reaches deep into the roots. The more profound the disconnect with the tradition, the greater the possibility of its renewal. To begin with, the criticisms need to be seen not as an affront of impiety from without but as internal questions for Christianity itself. What is more, the disconnect from tradition itself is something taking place within the tradition itself. As such, the full experience, with all the feelings of desperation that accompany it, needs to be faced resolutely. In this regard, Overbeck speaks directly to us today, both for his critical approach to the theology prevalent at the time and for the personal courage of his faith.

FALLING TO THE GROUND AND GETTING BACK UP

In the previous chapter, we challenged the self-serving vanity of a theology that tries to hold religion and science at bay by "domesticating"[19] the content of their critiques and translating their questions into terms familiar to its own apologetics. Inventions like the "theology of religions," for example, can be seen as an attempt to sedate the negative impact of religious pluralism. Similarly the construction of a "theology of nature" that aims to absorb the world view of natural science into a traditional Christian framework can be thought to prize its own opinions on science over the reality of science in the world today.

Such strategies are makeshift responses that fail to address the heart of the matter—like scratching one's shoe to relieve an itching foot, as the Chinese adage has it. Theologies of religion and theologies of nature treat religion and nature as objects external to Christianity, not as the inflammation of the faith they actually are. It is not a question of "problems" thrown at (προ-βαλεῖν) the Christian establishment from society at large. To the extent that religion and science are viewed by theology as an unknown, unfamiliar, and even ominous source of external problems, their solution lies in analyzing, interpreting, and finally domesticating the threat by defining it according to established theological conventions. The possibility of a deeper meaning is preempted on principle. Only by internalizing the problems and attending to the echoes of the unknown within the tradition itself can theology hope to understand what is happening to it. Christian faith and theology are themselves the problem. It is they that have been thrown to the ground by religion and science. The more fully theology confronts the claims of religion and science against it, the more it is obliged to accept its relocation to unfamiliar, *unheimlich* surroundings.

For more than two millennia, history and nature have been thought of as convenient locations for doing theology. Across ancient and medieval Christianity, and for a considerable period even after the scientific revolution of the sixteenth century, nature was a resource for demonstrating the truth of teachings about divine creativity. With the modern age, the Christian notion of revelation was reimagined as a higher rhythm breaking through the ordinary progression of time and history. As ideas of nature and history took a more decidedly anthropocentric turn, theology tried to follow suit, only to find its identity thrown into question. As nature and history grew in importance, they took on the role of "thought-stoppers." Theological reflection in its traditional form became increasingly marginalized as an impediment to progress. History ceased to be the *locus* of revelation. Instead of guaranteeing the absolute truth of the faith, history relativized it once and for all. Nature ceased to provide proof of divine creativity. Instead of conforming to the dictates of providence, nature came to be thought of as the domain of a ruthless, unbending law indifferent to the fate of human beings.

The term "thought-stopper" comes from Gregor Pence, an American bioethicist, who used it to characterize reactions to the birth of Dolly, the cloned sheep:

> The word "cloning" is a thought-stopper. Actually, even that statement is premature in that it implies that some thought was begun that has stopped.... The universal reaction has been Thou Shalt Not! Popular bioethicists measure how far down the slippery slope this event has brought us, and theologians warn of Playing God. People inveigh against medical technology as if the antibiotic they are now taking is not covered by this phrase.[20]

When the birth of Dolly was announced in February of 1997, it was met with a strong response from theology, ethics, and the rest of Christian academia. Dolly was born in 1996 under the supervision of a team of scientists at the Roslin Institute led by Ian Wilmut. They held off announcing the news for six months, until they could ascertain that the biotechnological "clone" was the same as sheep bred by ordinary procreation. The only difference they could determine was Dolly's manner of conception and birth. But, as Ted Peters, an American Lutheran theologian, pointed out, the questions being raised about Dolly went far beyond biology. To the Christian world, Dolly was nothing less than a living, breathing challenge to belief in God as creator:

> The moment cloning was announced, immediately and intuitively the world recognized that this is a theological issue. It's more than just science. It's more than just a new technological discovery. It's more than just an occasion for jokes about the name "Dolly" or, as found in the announcement appearing with the picture of two sheep on the cover of Time, "Will There Ever Be Another You?" (read "ewe"). This science raises religious questions, and the ambient anxiety raised ethical ire.[21]

As we noted earlier, Peters repeated the same error as the other Western theologians by characterizing the specifically Christian and theological reaction as generically "religious." In fact, other religions, like Buddhism, were all but silent in response to the event. Nearly every radical critique of the cloning of Dolly came from Judeo-Christian quarters. The very language of its accusations against creatures for attempting to "play God"[22] is meaningless for religions without an equivalent idea of God.

At any rate, Dolly was a *scandalum* for the Christian world, a stumbling block that stopped reflection on God, human beings, and the world in its tracks. The embryologist Ian Wilmut who earned fame worldwide for his scientific breakthrough, recognized instinctively that his work touched on the work of God, the Creator. He and his colleges published the account of their experience under the title *The Second Creation*. The subtitle clears up all doubt as to their aim: *Dolly and the Age of Biological Control*. Wilmut was convinced that Dolly "might reasonably claim to be the most extraordinary creature ever to be born."[23] The reason such a meek, unpretentious lamb could cause such a fright is not hard to see. Human beings are mammals like sheep, and if a sheep can be cloned, then in principle the same is possible for a human being. The lamb of God who was said to be a "stumbling block" and "foolishness" (1 Cor 1:23) to unbelievers in the early years of Christianity has met its counterpart in the twentieth century with the scandal and blasphemy of an innocent lamb named Dolly. That Wilmut and his colleges themselves understood Dolly's birth as a theological event is not insignificant. For a brief time, the web site of the Roslin Institute referred playfully—yet in all seriousness—to "progress AD," by which they meant not *anno Domini*, but "after Dolly." They saw themselves standing at the dawn on a new era where nothing was beyond the reach of biotechnological manipulation. It was as if Dolly, the little lamb, had put a spoke in a wheel that had rolled along unimpeded since the birth of the Lamb of God.

Slavoj Žižek brings an interesting perspective to the way theology deals with its embarrassment at questions raised by religion and science. He is sharply critical of conventional approaches to ethical problems raised by things like DNA manipulation and cloning, specifically because of their tendency to get bogged down in "hyphen-ethics" (*Bindenstrch-Ethik*). The moral questions swirling around bioethics should not be subjected to the constraints of applied ethics. Rather, they should open the way to novelty by way of the kind of "provisional ethics" that Descartes referred to in his *Discourse on Method*:

> When we engage on a new path, full of dangers and shattering new insights, we need to stick to old established rules as a practical guide for our daily lives, although we are well aware that the new insights will compel us to provide a fresh foundation for our entire ethical edifice.[24]

A provisional ethic, of course, "cannot replace the need for a thorough reflection of the emerging New," and this is precisely the predicament in which biogenetics puts us. Žižek's insight seems to me to apply directly to the applied theologies of "religion-theology" and "science-theology," which leave the Christian faith free "to stick to old established rules," even though "we are well aware that the new insights will compel us to provide a fresh foundation." At best, these hyphen-theologies are of provisional use.

In the conventional sense of the term, "bioethics" is taken to be a form of ethics in which general ethical theory is applied to a specific, traditional concept of *bios* (life). In current discussions of bioethics, however, it is not the general ethical principles that are being questioned, but the concept of life itself. In the debate over brain death, for example, it is the boundary between life and death itself that is up for question. In the same way, developments in biotechnology have forced ethics to back up and reconsider what counts as "life." By clinging to the conventional understanding of applied ethics, Žižek warns,

> what gets lost here, in this hyphen-ethics, is simply ethics as such. The problem is not that universal ethics gets dissolved in particular topics but, on the contrary, that particular scientific breakthroughs are directly confronted with the old humanist "values."[25]

As biological science breaks through one barrier after the other, the notion of life begins to look more and more fluid, and the possibility of constructing a stable bio-ethics ever more unlikely. Simply to take a new definition of life and incorporate it into the existing ethical framework would be like feeding hot coals to a snowman. This was in fact the pivotal point of the controversy between Habermas and Sloterdijke over cloning in the 1990s.[26]

The same holds true of attempts to cobble together a "science-theology" as a way to dispose of the problems science has thrown up to traditional theology, or a religion-theology to relieve the anxiety of religious pluralism. Religion and science cannot simply be hyphenated into theology as branches of "applied theology," because, as we argued in previous chapters, they are inherently inimical to the theological tradition. What choice does this leave us? Faced with earth-shattering breakthroughs like epoch-breaking phenomena like human cloning, Žižek suggests we "tarry with the negative":

> This, then, is the choice we are confronting today: either we choose the typically postmodern stance of reticence (let's not go the end, let's keep a proper distance toward the scientific Thing so that this Thing will not draw us into its black hole, destroying all our moral and human notions, or we dare to "tarry with the negative (*Verweilen beim Negativen*)," that is, we dare to fully assume the consequences of scientific modernity, with the wager that "our Mind is a genome" will also function as infinite judgment.[27]

Žižek alludes to the Preface of Hegel's *The Phenomenology of Mind*, where the mind is described as the power to "look the negative in the face, and dwell with it." The intrinsic life of the mind is only realized by facing death as "the most terrible thing" and "the greatest force of all." To turn away from death is to remain closed in on oneself, like the rest of nature. The mind becomes a concrete reality only by embracing the negative as the opposite within, that is, by "dwelling with it" or, as Žižek has it, by "tarrying with the negative."[28]

This suggests a way for theology to cope with controversies in the field of bioethics. The problems religion and science have thrown up to theology are experienced as something "negative" that shakes it to the foundations. Unless theology is prepared to betray its own nature as a hermeneutical endeavor to understand Christian faith in its actual historical circumstances, the possibility of doing theology in the traditional sense is negated. If theology simply appropriates the negative, it endorses the claims of religion and science that Christianity has come to an end—*finis christianismi*. It is caught in a dilemma from which it can neither advance nor retreat. Clearly, the only option for theology is to "look the negative in the face and dwell with it," to break through its own negation by penetrating to its core.

Christian faith has stumbled on religion and science, and fallen to the ground. The only way it can stand up again is to rely on religion and science, not to take a detour around the problems they represent but to break through them. It needs to sink to the bottom of the abyss that has opened at its feet through its confrontations with religion and science. Why not simply step around the obstacles and carry on as before? Because the historicism and naturalism that threaten Christianity resulted from a turn to science that was, at least in part, an outgrowth of the Christian faith itself. As a close reading of Troeltsch and Scheler shows, the revolutions in theology and anthropology that characterize the modern world were raised in the soil of Christianity. To think otherwise is to misunderstand the crisis.

The admonition of Zen Master Chinul (1158–1210), founder of Chogye Zen School in Korea, comes to mind. Those who seek an awakened mind, he says, do well to recall the words of the fourth Indian patriarch *Upagupta*;

> A person who falls to the ground gets back up by using that ground. To try to get up without relying on that ground would be impossible[29]

Chinul goes on to explain:

> Sentient beings are those who are deluded in regard to the one mind and give rise to boundless defilements. Buddhas are those who have awakened to the one mind and have given rise to boundless sublime functions. Although there

is a difference between delusion and awakening, essentially both derive from the one mind. Hence to seek Buddhahood apart from the mind is impossible.[30]

The "ground" of the awakened mind is the same mind that generates delusions blocking the way to Buddhahood or enlightenment. To awaken to one's Buddhahood is to realize that it is already in our nature, to break through the delusions of the mind by falling to the ground of the "one mind" that both darkens and enlightens. One must rely on the "one mind" to break through the delusions generated there. Robert Buswell, Chinul's English translator remarks:

> Since all defiled and pure dharmas derive from the one mind, sentient beings fall into the "dirt" (the defilements) of the "ground" (the one mind) when they ignorantly become involved with defiled sensual objects. Nevertheless, they must get up from this same ground to enter the pure realm of enlightenment. To raise themselves out of the morass of the defilements without relying on the mind-ground would be impossible.[31]

I have suggested that the Christian faith is being called to descend to the bottom of the abyss of the negative opened up by religion and science. Eventually, it will become apparent that there *is* no bottom, and from that point on, the descent reverses directions back to the surface. Drive down to the core of the earth and you will end up at the antipode of your starting point. When the "bottom" is seen to be the "core," the descent is transformed into ascent. We refer to it as a "breakthrough" because there is no solid ground at the turning point on which to take a secure foothold. Nishitani, whose thought we will take up in the following chapter, describes the experience of sinking into the abyss and discovering it as a turning point:

> "God is dead" can be understood in this sense. It opens an abyss within life, before which we can no longer say that we live in the presence of God or in the love of God, that we are dead to ourselves and living in God, that we live in union with God, and so forth. Nietzsche once remarked, "If you look into the abyss long enough, the abyss will look back at you."[32]

We look the negative in the face and the negative looks back at us, and from that moments we can no longer distinguish the two. To paraphrase Meister Eckhart, we may say that the eye with which we see the negative is the same eye with which the negative sees us.[33] The breakthrough occurs in the realization that the abyss is the ground of our existence and, at the same time, that we are the ground of the abyss. Whether or not theologians will find a suitable way of responding to the challenges religion and science depends on whether or not their faith is prepared to "tarry" at the experience of having its foundations overturned and rely on religion and science to reveal a breakthrough.

THE CHANNEL FORMS AS THE WATER FLOWS

The way through the negative is to meet it head on and dwell in it, to give oneself over to the flow of the negative and ride it out. If theology is to break through its current crisis of identity, it must be prepared to embrace the rhetoric of the negative. The place for doing theology is defined by the experience of truth as interpretation and its expression as self-negation. Raimon Panikkar's reflections on interreligious dialogue offer a concrete model for understanding religion and science as theological topics.

Panikkar, a seminal thinker whose theological contributions to the dialogue among religions have been pivotal, opened his book *The Intrareligious Dialogue* with a chapter entitled "The Rhetoric of the Dialogue." There he proposed five "attitudes" towards other religions—exclusivism, inclusivism, parallelism, interpenetration, and pluralism—and five "models" for engagement—geographical, physical, geometrical, anthropological, and mystical. This is not the place to examine each of the categories separately but only to note that Panikkar does not employ them in order to "elaborate a theory of the religious encounter." On the contrary, he insists that they are instead part of the encounter itself and affect its rhetoric:

> And it is out of this praxis that I would like to propose the following attitudes and models for the proper rhetoric in the meeting of religious traditions. I do not elaborate now on the value of these attitudes or the merits of these models. This would require studying the function and nature of the metaphor as well as developing a theory of the religious encounter. I only describe some attitudes and models, although I will probably betray my sympathies in the form of critical considerations.[34]

Panikkar's attitudes and models are not imposed on interreligious dialogue from without but emerge from its practice in the concrete. Their adoption is determined by how naturally they respond to the needs of those in dialogue and their respective traditions. In his words, this amounts to a demand for "*adequate rhetoric—in the classical sense of the word.*"[35] The rhetoric he has in mind is not, of course, empty flattery aimed at camouflaging the truth but a tool for persuasion. We took this up in Chapter 1, where we pointed to the oratorical skills required deal to properly with a given *topic*. According to Aristotle, the classical elements of rhetoric are invention, arrangement, style, memory, and delivery. For Panikkar, what is true of speech and writing also holds for communication among religious traditions in dialogue.

Panikkar's emphasis on the role of rhetoric stems from his insistence that dialogue is essential for particular religions to understand what it means to coexist with a plurality of religions and to persuade others to appreciate their respective modes of self-understanding. Understanding and persuasion are two sides of the same coin here. Interpretation carried out in dialogue requires its own rhetoric to express the meaning of what is understood, a unique *elocutio* that refuses to reduce differences of religious experience to a single common ground or language for expression. There is no neutral standpoint for comparison, "no fulcrum outside" from which to generalize about the plurality of faiths. As Panikkar puts it:

> We cannot compare (*comparare*—that is, to treat on an equal—*par*—basis). We can only *imparare*—that is, learn from the other to a dialogical dialogue that does not seek to win or to convince, but to search together from our different vantage points.

Panikkar speaks of authentic dialogue between religions as a "dialogical dialogue,"[36] that is, one that conforms to the nature of understanding itself. Dialogical dialogue is an ongoing process of understanding oneself in front of the other, and in this means persuading the other and being persuaded in return:

> Understanding is not a function of our mind triggered by the outside world but an act that involves our whole being. In that sense, it is almost an inversion, a move toward wholeness, a turn towards a more encompassing and therefore more universal sphere of being, a higher and broader truth, an openness to fulfillment. I will never be able to understand if I remain on my own fixed standpoint. I must "move inwards" to encompass what lies beyond me. Not only does

the object dissolve in an act of true understanding, but the subject changes and moves—towards the whole: a true, genuine act of being convinced by having been moved by a higher truth; a reversal that moves forward by stopping and motivates us to understand more and more.[37]

To understand is to be persuaded, subdued, and overwhelmed (*überwältigt*) by what has been understood. In this sense, the only authentic *topos* for doing theology is that of dialogical dialogue, which

> is not only a religious endeavor for the participants, it is a genuine *locus theologicus*, to speak in Christian Scholastic parlance, a source in itself of religious (theological) understanding. A theory of a particular religion today has also to deal with other religions. We can no longer ignore the other. The religions of others—our neighbors—becomes a religious question for us, for our religion.[38]

Engaging in dialogical dialogue is a testimony to our commitment to understand ourselves through encounter with the other, to our insight that we are interwoven epistemologically and ontologically with the other, and to our openness to mutual persuasion through mutual self-understanding. In a word, it is a concrete expression of the awakening to the reciprocal interpenetration of self and other. This is a far cry from any "noble effort at reducing the immense variety of human experience to one single and common language."[39] Quite the opposite, it is aware that "each encounter creates a new language."[40] The idea of a *locus theologicus*, which derives from medieval scholasticism,[41] entails a particular way of speaking or using words suited to the circumstances in which theology is being carried out. The interreligious dialogue demands nothing less.

Insofar as hermeneutics touches on the aesthetic experience of understanding in a way that self-evident scientific axioms cannot, it is only natural that it should draw on rhetoric as a vehicle of expression. As Gadamer remarked in this regard, expression is never merely a matter of personal preference. It is determined by the content of what is being communicated and the context in which that content is understood. The specific "topic" towards which the rhetorical arts are directed, therefore, must include both the hermeneutical experience of truth and its expression to others. His aim is to the original meaning of *expressio* as an enunciation that leaves an impression on the listeners in virtue of something present behind the words, not because of anything the speaker brings to it. "To find a good expression is to find an expression which aims at a certain impression; it is in no sense an expression of one's personal experience."[42] To paraphrase what Curtius had to say the source of a "historical topic," the expression flows naturally out of the dialogue and into the quill of the participants. This is true of all dialogue, but when the participants speak from a particular religious tradition, Panikkar observes, they need to accept their expression also as "the proper use of a divine gift" and "cultivation of that precious divine gift that Man has."[43]

Our concern in this chapter has been with understanding the "negative" that religion and science have imposed on Christian theology and learning how to dwell in it until the way to a breakthrough is revealed. The readiness to respond to the theological imperative to dialogue with religion and science head-on, rather than seek a detour around the problem requires, on the one hand, that we identify the "negative," and on the other, that we adopt a language suited our experience of it. Rhetoric is determined by interpretation, not the other way around.

Heinrich Ott's commentary on the theological legacy of Franz Overbeck underscores the point. In particular, he drew attention to Overbeck's mistreatment of the Buddhist tradition in his overall critique of liberal theology. For Ott, it is not only a question of the theological judgments themselves but also of the style in which they are expressed:

> The little that Overbeck wrote about Buddhism he based on what he knew of its teachings, not on firsthand accounts. This is true of his contemporaries as well. We are today the first generation of theologians to be confronted with *living* Buddhism *to the full* (not simply marginally, like those in the mission fields), that is, with the actual thinking of Buddhists as partners in conversation. It has become impossible for us to do theology seriously without taking this into consideration. By theology, I do not mean merely negotiating a way to be accepted by those in power—unlike the Wilhelmine era in Germany, such efforts would likely be futile in today's situation!—but theology in the sense (and *style*!) of an honest attempt at communication.... How are we to talk about history and eschatology, for example, without taking into account what Buddhist teachings have to say on the matter?[44]

Furthermore, as one of the first theologians to acknowledge the importance of Heidegger's philosophy for theology, Ott focuses on the "change of the style" (*Stilveränderung*)[45] that affected a turn of thought in his later writing. Ott agrees with Karl Löwith's assessment that Heidegger's philosophy suddenly lost clarity and became difficult to understand both in content and in style. Rather than proceed logically and go directly to the point, he gets sidetracked in qualifications and variant approaches. His writing moves forwards and backwards repeatedly, sometimes with the aid of poetic language, leading Ott to question whether changes in his thinking might not be due fundamentally to his change of style. Heidegger's *Kehre* is said to have begun with his inaugural lecture at the University of Freiburg in 1929, "What is Metaphysics?," in which he discussed

> the meaning of *nothingness* for human existence.... Existence runs up against nothingness. It encounters nothingness through the feeling of fear. It experiences nothingness in a such a way that nothingness is understood as something that has always been present at the bottom of existence. Existence also experiences nothingness as something that makes existence "confront itself" and "confront that which exists.[46]

As is well known, Heidegger's direct reference to nothingness (*das Nichts*) was meant as a criticism of Western metaphysics since Aristotle, for having treated Being as a "thing." Since *Being and Time* he had been arguing that Being be viewed as the self-understanding of the human being as *Dasein*, being-there. This, in turn, meant confronting death as the end of one's being. In his Freiburg lecture he penetrates deeper into this same insight by suggesting the encounter with nothingness as a way to overcome the objectification of being:

> That to which the relation to the world refers are beings themselves—and nothing besides.
> That from which every attitude takes its guidance are beings themselves—and nothing further.
> That with which the scientific confrontation in the irruption occurs are beings themselves—and beyond that nothing.[47]

According to Heidegger, modern science, like metaphysics, has looked on Being as an object and disregarded nothingness as the mere privation of Being. Their only interest is in beings and nothing else. They have discarded the question of nothingness as useless for understanding the world.

But Heidegger asks whether the addition of the phrase "nothing else" (*sonst nichts*) does not prove that nothingness already has a place in our understanding of being. With the question, "What about this nothing?" Heidegger's thinking begins to change course and include nothingness as a given in human existence. His attention turns to the origins of being by turning away from its objectifying and presentational modes to recalling and recollection. If the meaning of being leads us to the meaning of a nothingness hidden at the ground of being, then it also radiates back to the source from our very inquiry into being. This, Ott concludes, is why Heidegger's writing cannot proceed in a straight line but only through a continued advance and regress.[48]

Heidegger's *Kehre* speaks directly to our concern with the "negative" that affronts theology through its encounter with science and religion not as an object blocking the road ahead but as something at the very ground of theology itself. The negative drives theology back to its foundation where the question of the negative can radiate back to the encounter with science and religion that occasioned it. It is as if the theologian were positioned between facing mirrors reflecting back and forth on each other. There is no way for theology to express the experience of the assault of the negative from without but to acknowledge it at work within. *Regressus est egressus, egressus est regressus*—this is the only style suited to the nature of the negative.

Dialogue is the proper *locus* for theology to break through the problem that religion and science represent for the Christian faith by having recourse to religion and science. One enters by understanding the other and exits by expressing a new self-understanding. Having fallen to the ground, one breaks through the ground to regain a footing in the real world.

As we have been insisting from the outset, the Christian faith is already entangled at the roots with religion and science. It is not so that we have faith, and then, on the basis of that faith, decide to dialogue with religion and science. To be conscious of one's faith is to know that it is already radically affected by religion and science. They represent the irreversible hermeneutical situation within which faith must seek understanding. The illusion that faith can think on its own apart from the dialogue with religion and science is like standing under the midday sun and wondering what daylight is like. Let us be clear: dialogue makes faith possible; dialogue is already the exercise of faith. Christianity's dialogue with religion and science is a dialogue with something inside the faith, not a one-sided reaction to an external stimulus. We hear the voice of the other only as it reverberates from within the faith. In the hearing, voice and echo are indistinguishable.

I find Martha Nussbaum's talk of an "organic connection" between form and contents[49] a good way of thinking about the intrinsic relationship between the content of the Christian encounter with religion and science and its expression. Of the bond between literature and philosophy, she remarks that "literary form is not separable from philosophical content." Style is not an empty vessel into which contents can be poured. It is already "a part of content—an integral part, then, of the search for and the statement of truth.... Style itself makes its claims, expresses its sense of what matters."[50] Nussbaum's description of the nature of style reminds us Merleau-Ponty's remark in an essay on "Metaphysics and the Novel":

> The work of a great novelist always rests on two or three philosophical ideas.... The function of the novelist is not to state these ideas thematically but to make them exist for us in the way that things exist. Stendhal's role is not to hold forth on subjectivity; it is enough that he make it present.[51]

Since the end of the nineteenth century, philosophy and literature have drawn closer together as "just different expressions" of how we approach the world. Their methods do not coincide. Philosophy prefers to state ideas "thematically," whereas literature aims at making ideas "exist for us in the way that things exist," which requires a distinct style of expression. Merleau-Ponty supports the claim with Pascal's claim that metaphysics "is present... in the heart's slightest movement."[52] Whether it be literary, theological, or philosophical, style is the heart's response to what touches it from the outside. It is like a board with a thick layer of dust on it. Tap it along the sides or from the bottom and different patterns form. So it is with the heart and its style.

Nussbaum draws on two analogies of literary style from Henry James's *The Golden Bowl*: "expressive plants" and "perceiving angels." Regarding the first, James likens style to "a plant that grows out of that soil and expresses, in its forms, the soil's character and composition." In this mode, style is a function of literary content, for "just as the plant emerges from the seeded soil, taking its form from the combined character of seed and soil, so the novel and its terms flower from and express the conceptions of the author, his or her sense of what matters."[53] In the second mode, "perceiving angels," novelists alert us to "winged creatures" and "some creatures of the air, perhaps birds, perhaps angels," that make us ascend this gloomy world. In the one case, style is rooted in the earth and absorbs its nutrition. In the other, it lifts us up and away from the earth where we can connect with the divine.

If we grant the "organic connection" between content and style, what style is best suited to the expression of the faith in dialogue with religion and science? Its style must flow from the content and express it, but at the same time, it must interpret the content.

Authentic dialogue does not allow for any theory or method to decide matters of style a priori. As the ancient saying goes, "the channel forms as the water flows."[54] The image is that of a stream of water that does not flow into a conduit dug out in advance but it flows across the land freely, cutting its own channel as it goes; or of a rushing stream that overflows its banks and spreads out into new tributaries. By entering into dialogue, Christianity foregoes exclusive control of the style of its self-expression. As the dialogue unfolds, the proper style "flows into the author's quill" of its own accord. A theology that is conscious of having been shaped by the encounter with religion and science cries out for further phenomenological analysis. Like a geologist digging through the layers of material deposited over time, the theologian needs to map the strata that lay beneath the ground of theology today. The Italian philosopher Enzo Paci offers a striking analogy based on tracing a simple lump of burning coal to its prehistoric roots:

> At each instant we perceive, because at each instant we live that which for the intellect is a paradox: the consumption of our life, which is new life. But, precisely because we perceive it, it is necessary for the past that we consume, like the coal produced by the amalgamation of the forests of the Paleozoic era, to be a reality; for that past, which formed them and gave rise to them, consumed them and killed them, and finally transformed them into coal, to have been a reality. And it is in fact this very reality which we perceive: the perception of the heat that today warms me is also the perception of the reality of those forests which lived before me, about three hundred million years before man appeared on earth. And if I do not dogmatize my perception into an abstract discourse, I feel, even when I do not know what it was, that there has been an existence on earth before man, an existence before what we usually call life, an existence which has always been preceded by another existence. Another exis-

tence before mine, before man's life, before the existence of the earth, of the solar system, of the galaxies. Perhaps because of this, today I can feel as mine the existence of what is other than I.[55]

In the following chapter, we turn to the content of theology's dialogue with Buddhism and science. A discussion of the style that emerges from that dialogue will be taken up in the final chapter, but only in general terms. As important as the development of a suitable and concrete theological rhetoric is for the dialogue with religion and science, it falls outside the scope of this book.[56]

4

The *Topos* of *Śūnyatā*

We have been arguing that theology today is faced with the live, forced, and momentous task of overcoming its own negation at the hands of religion and science. At first glance, its encounter with "the negative" appears to be the result of external threats against which the faith must defend itself. On closer reflection, it became clear that problem reaches deeper into the core of theology and shakes the very foundations of its claim to understand and express itself rationally. In such circumstances, theology cannot simply ignore or otherwise try to cope with the forces that seem to negate it. If there is a way through the crisis, it can only begin by accepting the negative as part of its own identity.

To pure this thought further, I would like to draw on the writings of the Buddhist philosopher Nishitani Keiji (1900–1990),[1] a pivotal thinker in the Kyoto school that crystallized around the towering figure of Nishida Kitarō (1870–1945), who sought to fuse the insights of Zen Buddhism with Western religious and philosophical thought. I will single out Nishitani's 1961 book, *Religion and Nothingness*, for special attention in that it attempts to construct a Buddhist philosophy of emptiness integrated with Christian thought—the mystical tradition in particular—and alert us to the concerns of modern science. The question we bring to Nishitani's work is whether and to what extent his particular Buddhist perspective might shed light on our discussion of the relationship among Christianity, religion, and science, which has become a defining problem for theology today. To begin with, however, it may help to clarify the reasons for turning to Nishitani for philosophical guidance.

First of all, it is worth recalling that Nishitani's "standpoint of emptiness (*śūnyatā*)"[2] grew out of his personal struggles as reflected in his serious reading of Nietzsche's nihilism and its influence on Martin Heidegger's philosophy.[3] Nishitani traced the source of Nietzsche's nihilistic thinking to his positive reception of modern science and its annihilation of the system of values undergirding the Christian worldview, leading him finally to announce the death of God. Nihilism deprives existence of any permanent, substantial ground, including what has traditionally been referred to as "God." For Nishitani, the fact that nihilism has taken away the ultimate ground of human existence needs to be accepted, inversely, as the ground of existence. Indeed, the possibility of such an inversion is already contained within nihilism itself. By accepting the self-overcoming of nihilism, we break through it. Nihilism has dispensed with all hope of rescue from without. There is no other way to get over nihilism than to meet it head-on and at bottom.

The logic that drives Nishitani's approach to nihilism can be found at work throughout his writing. James Heisig sees it as a defining "pattern" of thought that "is present already in the essay he wrote on Nietzsche and Eckhart while with Heidegger in Germany, in which he sees that nihilistic despair is overcome not from without but from within nihilism itself, at its depth."[4] I take Heisig's remarks on the defining character of Nishitani's philosophy as a direct endorsement of my decision to enlist his thinking as a guide to breaking through "the negative" with which religion and science have beset Christian theology:

> As we have seen with so many of the other ideas Nishitani takes up—nihilism, self, interpersonal relationship, ethics, science, history—Nishitani neither simply rejects traditional ideas he wants to rethink nor does he simply modify them in the light of his own standpoint. Rather, he tries to think ideas through to the point where they collapse before what they are trying to express, and at the point of collapse disclose what had been neglected. What he calls "breakthrough" always implies a rebirth, not only of the self but also of that which has been broken through.[5]

As the term "breakthrough" indicates, Nishitani's struggles with nihilism were never only a question of academic curiosity. Looking back over his life as a philosopher, Nishitani confessed that no word captured "the starting point of his philosophy" as well as "nihilism." Again, he did not mean a philosophical concept or a pessimistic cast of mind, but "something prior to philosophy and at the same time essentially including a move to a philosophical dimension."[6] He saw it as a fundamental and "long-lasting mood"[7] that affected his view of reality and begged for rational expression. To cite Heisig again, it was "a nihilistic despair over the human condition" that spread out into "doubt over all of existence." Nishitani's philosophy was an attempt to direct this doubt to "ascend to the wonder of emptiness" as understood by the Buddhist idea of *śūnyatā*. His approach reads like a paraphrase of Chinul's admonition mentioned in the previous chapter: "One who has fallen to the ground because of nihilism gets back up with the help of that nihilism. Without relying on nihilism, one cannot stand back up." Nishitani's logic of "breakthrough" applies directly to our insistence that "the negative" be taken up as a genuine theological problem and not simply skirted as a passing intellectual fad.

A second reason for our interest in Nishitani's thought has to do with its contents, which took shape through active dialogue with Christian thought and natural science. What is more, he saw the standpoint of *śūnyatā* as opening a new perspective on the relationship between religion and science. In this connection, he introduced the notions of "double exposure" and "circuminsessional interpenetration"[8] to complement his logic of breakthrough. We shall have more to say of this later. Suffice it to note for now that Nishitani's unique place within the Kyoto School, as his translator Jan Van Bragt has written, is characterized by a "constant preoccupation with nihilism, and its alliance with scientism, that is undermining the very foundations of Western civilization, leaving man with no place to stand as man."[9]

Thus with regard to both method and content, Nishitani's philosophical standpoint is structured around a three-way dialogue with Buddhism, Christianity, and modern science. Against the backdrop of modern nihilism and scientific progress, he attempted to reformulate any number of traditional ideas, among them the Christian idea of a personal God. The following passage confirms the overlap with the central problematic of this book:

> Modern science has completely transformed the old view of nature, resulting in the birth of various forms of atheism and the fomenting of an indifference to religion in general.... This turn of events can hardly be without relevance to the question of God as it affects all religions, but in particular as it affects the kind

of clearly defined theism we find in Christianity. Until the problem of religion and science reaches a level that is fundamental enough to render the approach to the question of God itself problematical, we cannot say that the issue has really been faced. It is as serious as that.[10]

In short, I am persuaded that Nishitani's analysis of our present situation and his dialogical method of response can throw light on the way ahead for a self-understanding of the faith suffering from the increasing irrelevance of theology today.

SCIENCE, NIHILISM, AND THE TRUE SELF

The seeds of Nishitani's philosophy, as we have seen, were planted in the soil of nihilism. He recognized in Nietzsche's declaration of the "death of God" the extent to which the highest values of human existence had been obliterated by the mechanical worldview of modern science. He understood the screams of the "madman" lamenting the darkness at noon: "How could we drink up the sea? Who gave us the sponge to wipe away the entire horizon?"[11] The elimination of all traces of God from the world and the general indifference to human beings that mark modern science are symptoms of a broader malaise that Nishitani calls the experience of "nihility." At the same time, nihility is the very place at which we can experience the "ecstatic transcendence" of nihility:

> Only when a man has felt such an abyss open at the ground of his existence does his subjectivity become subjectivity in the true sense of the word: only then does he awaken to himself as truly free and independent.[12]

For Nishitani, the nihility resulting from the assault on traditional values by modern science is not a dead end but a creative starting point for a new understanding of religion and human beings. Insofar as the scientific explanation of nature must eventually turn back on the way we understand ourselves as part of nature, the nihilism caused by science can be embraced as an invitation to deeper self-understanding. Nishitani has cut to the heart of the matter here. To borrow Žižek's expression, his counsel to "tarry with" nihilism lays open the traditional Buddhist concept of *śūnyatā* as a new horizon against which to understand religion, science, and human beings.

The standpoint of emptiness that Nishitani constructed as a response to nihilism needs to be seen as part of the overall search for what he called "elemental subjectivity," or what Buddhism calls the "true self." That is to say, the thought processes involved in overcoming nihilism require that we appropriate nihilism subjectively in what Nishitani referred to as "scientific conscience." He likens this to Buddhism's idea of the "great doubt" that precedes awakening to one's true self.

Nishitani's concern with subjectivity is reflected already in the title of his first book, *A Philosophy of Elemental Subjectivity*, a collection of essays published in 1949. The volume opens with a comparison of the nihilism of Nietzsche's Zarathustra and the mysticism of Meister Eckhart, both of which sought authentic subjectivity in detachment from what lies outside the self. Nishitani goes on to propose elemental subjectivity as the essence of religion: "When all attachment to objects is broken, the fixed image of the self is also broken. At that point, from the opposite direction, the connection between the self and the ground of life begins to disclose itself."[13] Nishitani likens Eckhart's *Ohne Warum* to Nietzsche's "God is dead" in the sense that both signal a radical detachment from something external thought to be the ground of the self. For both, the true ground of human beings and ultimate reality is one and the same: an abyss before which we can come to radical, elemental subjectivity.

For Nishitani, Eckhart's mysticism, together with Nietzsche's nihilism, marked a milestone in explaining the true meaning of subjectivity. For Eckhart, the ground of the soul is no different from the ground of God. Only by breaking through the idea of God as an objective person can the soul reach the ground of the personal God, namely, the Godhead that can be understood neither as person nor a non-person. In this breakthrough, the soul comes to the awareness of its own ground as one with the ground of God. Thus, the soul is reborn as an elemental subjectivity, dependent on nothing, thorough a double negation—affirmation by the negation of a negation. First, the soul is denied its ground in a personal God, throwing it into an abyss of nihility. Second, by negating nihility and breaking through the bottom of that abyss, the soul arrives at the abyss of the personal God, the Godhead, where it is reborn as a radically free subject who is no longer merely autonomous nor heteronymous. Elsewhere Nishitani remarks apropos of this process of affirmation through negation:

> Eckhart pointed to such a standpoint in explaining the "essence" of the personal God as absolute nothingness. He conceived of it as the kind of field of absolute negativity that even breaks through subjectivity (in the sense of the personality) as something lying directly underfoot of our subjectivity, and at the same time as the kind of field of absolute affirmation on which our personality also becomes manifest. In a word, he took it as a field of absolute death-*sive*-life.[14]

Nishitani leaves no doubt that his idea of subjectivity is closer to the Christian mystical tradition than it is to the modern idea of the human person. He writes apropos of Eckhart:

> The ground of God is the ground of the self and the ground of the self is the ground of God. It is the self that attains complete freedom and transcendental religious insight. In other words, when this medieval German mystic speaks of a "breakthrough," he is expressing an elemental subjectivity that transcends the idea of a God opposed to the self in a personal sense and thus arrives at its own self-awareness.[15]

In this context, Nishitani's claim that "nihilism teaches us to return to our forgotten selves and to reflect on traditional Oriental culture,"[16] implies, on the one hand, that the European nihilism that came to its climax in Nietzsche prepares the way for an *elemental subjectivity* in the sense of "something completely *without foundation* in outside authority, divine law, or faith."[17] On the other hand, it implies that the burden of Western nihilism can be shouldered by the Buddhist idea *śūnyatā*, whose practice leads to the enlightenment of the true self.

Nishitani's remark on the recovery of "our forgotten selves" is a clear reference to his own experience of nihility and subsequent radical "subjectivization of atheism." In the preface to *The Self-Overcoming of Nihilism*, he makes it clear that his inquiry into nihilism was prompted by his sympathy for the nihilist who "represents a history of the all-out struggle of subjectivity against domination or suppression by something outside of subjectivity." In this sense, his concern is with the self-overcoming of what is "usually called nihilism."[18] It is a kind of nihilism turned against nihilism, an inversion and deepening of "unconscious nihilism," which is no more than a superficial rejection of religious and metaphysical values. Its aim is a "conscious nihilism" or positive reception of the nihility at the ground of one's existence.[19]

The existential adoption of nihilism and the subsequent awakening of subjectivity is closely related to the modern scientific view of nature in whose backwash nihilism emerged. In an essay on "Science and Zen," Nishitani remarks:

> For a thinker who faces science existentially, i.e., who accepts it as a problem for his existence as such, that the usual state of the universe is explained by science in terms of lifeless materiality means that the universe is a field of existential death for himself and for all mankind.

For Nishitani, the existential question natural science has raised for human beings and their self-understanding coincides with the general assessment of Christian theology that the world as natural science sees it is "a field in which one is obliged..., 'to abandon oneself and throw away one's own life,' a field of absolute negation."[20] It is a world of death in which everything is predetermined, with no possibility of change or hope for a future different from the past. It is a world governed by the law of cause and effect: the future is the effect, the past is the cause. The religious awakening to the world as a "vanity of vanities" is a direct rejection of "the dead nature"[21] in which things are always the same. Insofar as we are part of the natural world, our lives, too, are permeated by death. What, then, can it mean to accept this "absolute negation" as the ground of our existence?

Nishitani singles out Schopenhauer, Kierkegaard, and Feuerbach as marking the transition from realism to nihilism. Aside from chapters devoted to Stirner, Russian nihilists, and Heidegger, the bulk of *The Self-Overcoming of Nothingness* is given to an analysis of Nietzsche's nihilism. I would like to draw special attention to his evaluation of Nietzsche's "experimental knowledge" (*cognitio experimentalis*) as an attempt to embrace science existentially. As we noted above, science for Nishitani is more than a systematic means for accumulating knowledge of the world. It determines and reflects the way we exist as human beings. Therefore, question of science is not just a question about science. Rather, it is the questioner who has become the object of the question. Nishitani cites Nietzsche's *On the Genealogy of Morals* (III.25):

> Has the self-diminution of the human being, its *will* to self-diminution, not progressed inexorably since Copernicus? Alas, the faith in human worth, its uniqueness and indispensability in the rank-order of creation has gone—the human has become an *animal*, literally an animal, without reservation or qualification; the human, who formerly believed itself to be almost divine ("child of god," "God-man"). Since Copernicus, humanity seems to have got itself on to a sloping plane—already sliding faster and faster away from the center—into what? into nothingness? into the *"piercing* feeling of its own nothingness"? That's fine! this would be just the right way—into the *old* ideal?[22]

The radical fearlessness of Nietzsche's existential appropriation of science as a "scientific conscience" stands visibly in the background of his nihilism. The function of nihilism as a "mode of existence in which one relates to and overcomes oneself" is no different from the way science works to explain all phenomena in the world by relying solely on its own principles. Nietzsche's nihilism goes hand in glove with his existential commitment to natural science to create a single "scientific-existential standpoint."[23] Nietzsche identified his own self so completely with the determinative powers of nature that nature no longer exercised control over him from the outside. The self became one with destiny through an all-embracing *amor fati*, a mode of self-understanding in which one loves one's own fate without despairing over the absence of divine providence or yielding to simple fatalism:

> Every action of the self in this context is influenced by all things and in turn influences all things. All things become the fate of the self, and the self becomes the fate of all things. At such a fundamental level the world moves at one with the self, and the self moves at one with the world.[24]

When we embrace our own fate lovingly, we are able to endure the eternal recurrence of things without the vain expectation of something absolutely "new" like a new world set in motion by the *parousia Christi*. Nietzsche's idea of "eternal recurrence of the same thing" (*die ewige Wiederkehr des Gleichen*) cements his identification with nature in contrast to the hope for a second coming of Christ that will usher in "a new heaven and new earth" (Rev 21:1). In short, the "scientific conscience" is the true source of nihilism, whose aim is "to strive scientifically for full understanding of all phenomena of the world—including the world within."[25] When all is said and done, Nietzsche's way of approaching science and its mechanistic worldview led him to see "every problem in the modern age as a problem of the honesty and conscience of the self."[26] Consequently, system of values based on Christianity is doomed to fade away with the existential appropriation of science.[27]

Nietzsche was well aware that the problem of natural science did not emerge by chance. It had been simmering in history at the ground of the self, where it was part of our self-understanding even before it boiled over into nihilism. The nihilism that religion promises to overcome through recourse to a higher, eternal reality is little more than a despair at the meaningless of life on earth. The nihility that served Nishitani as a philosophical starting point remained after religion had done what it could. Here, paradoxically, is where nihility first becomes a genuine religious problem. That is to say, nihilism appears in full force when not only the realm of finite beings (the world of "phenomena") is negated as fundamentally vacuous, but when the realm of eternal being (the world of "essences" conceived as a transcendent alternative) is also negated. Through this double negation the finite and the infinite dissolve together into the backdrop of nothingness. Finitude becomes full and final.[28]

Let us be clear what Nishitani means by this "double negation." First, it is nihilism's rejection of naive ideas of the infinity of the world and acceptance of the ultimate vanity and futility of all things. But the negation does not stop there. The real meaning of nihilism only comes into relief when the hope of a higher, eternal realm that embraces the world and gives it meaning is rejected as an illusion. In line with his claim that nihilism leads us back to our forgotten selves and a reconsideration of traditional culture, Nishitani relates this double negation to the Buddhist way of enlightenment. He identified three interlocking themes in *The Self-Overcoming of Nihilism*: Nietzsche, Dostoevsky—"The figures of Nietzsche and Dostoevsky burned a lasting impression deep into my soul... and the tremors I experienced at that time have continued to make my heart tremble ever since"[29]—and Buddhist emptiness. Despite his comment that "the final theme, of Buddhist 'emptiness,' came to capture my interest more gradually," it is not difficult to see how it also affected his reading of Dostoevsky and Nietzsche.[30]

Actually, in a 1985 interview Nishitani admitted that he was surprised to find how many Zen terms he had used in his undergraduate thesis, including a saying about an"old mirror"[31] he inserted at the end. But even without the use of Zen language, the role that nihilism played as a point of departure for his philosophy has all the markings of a *kōan* aimed at the discovery of the true self. He describes the state of mind that led him to begin practicing Zen on Kyoto's Shōkoku-ji:

> I was understanding something, but it was unrelated to myself. I felt very strange. I felt as if I were dangling in the air. The best way I can put it is my feet weren't planted firmly on the ground. The soles of my feet weren't touching ground. There was a gap. In German there is a term *schweben*, which means unsteady, no place to rest. It's kind of like floating.[32]

As his doubts about the existence and meaning of the self were left to deepen, they were transformed into an all-encompassing "great doubt"[33] in which the hope finding an answer in religion was itself called into question:

> Nihilism includes in its essence a doubt which possesses an irrepressible defi-ance of ethics and religion.... Thus one doubts any attempt to find meaning in human life, especially through ethics or religion.

Through his own experience, he had come to see that the only way to *over-come* nihilism is "by *going through* it," that breaking through the bottom of nihilism brings one to "the essence of nihilism."[34] This is how he understood what Zen calls "the self-presentation of the great doubt."[35]

By characterizing nihilism as great doubt, Nishitani located it within the landscape of the Buddhist quest of the true self, that is, of an authen-tic subjectivity in which "the being of the self is revealed to the self itself as something groundless."[36] The attainment of such a state is the very thing Zen is pointing at with expressions like "In the Great Death heaven and earth become new" and "Beneath the Great Death, the Great Enlightenment." In a word, once he had linked nihilism with the problem of the true self, he had found a starting point of philosophy that was true to his own experience:

> If nihilism is anything, it is first of all a problem of the self. And it becomes such a problem only when the self becomes a problem, when the ground of the existence called "self" becomes a problem for itself.[37]

For Nietzsche, the way to the self's becoming a problem unto itself was the realization that faith in God as an eternal ground for the self turned out to be a historically conditioned construction of the mind:

> What had once been considered transhistorical now began to be seen as prod-
> ucts of history. With this an abyssal nihility opened up at the ground of his-
> tory and self-being, and everything turned into a question mark.... Metaphysics
> itself became a problem of history and of the epoch itself. The eternal inquiry
> into what it means to be a self was transfigured into an inquiry into historical
> actuality, and Existence became *fundamentally* historical.[38]

Nihilism, as well as Nishitani's attempts to overcome it, was no less a historical phenomena, the chief of whose conditions was "the mutual antago-
nism between religion and science." As commentators on his thought have
noted, the way to understanding his "standpoint of emptiness" begins with
an inquiry into the relation between nihilism and science.[39] Nishitani likens
it to the first stage existence as set out in Nietzsche's *Zarathustra*:

> From this point on, Existence as nihilism begins. The bearing of burdens, rev-
> erence; and cultivation through the religious or philosophical life represent a
> preparatory stage. The transformation into the camel, the first stage on the path
> to wisdom, involves both immersing oneself in the teachings of traditional reli-
> gion and metaphysics as well as a turn to nihilism which breaks through them.
> It involves what was spoken of earlier as a turn to the unconscious nihilism at
> the core of religion and metaphysics, and from there to true, conscious nihil-
> ism. The stimulus for this turn, that which drives the camel into the desert, is
> provided by the virtues of honesty and truthfulness cultivated by the morality
> of religion.[40]

RELIGION AND SCIENCE AT THE STANDPOINT OF EMPTINESS

Nishitani's philosophy, as we have seen, begins by staring into the
nihilistic abyss opened by the modern scientific view of the world. Christianity's experience in this regard has been particularly distressing not only
because of its overtly antagonistic attitude toward the natural sciences, but
also because it represents the historical background against which they
developed. The problem of nihilism, Nishitani argues, smouldered "hidden"
beneath the surface of this conflict until at last it flamed up in modern con-

sciousness.[41] In this sense, nihilism offers "a new angle"[42] from which to view the relationship between science and religion:

> I am convinced that the problem of nihilism lies at the root of the mutual aversion between religion and science, and it is here that my philosophical engagement found its starting point, and from which my preoccupation with nihilism grew larger until it enveloped almost everything.[43]

Nishitani's approach to religion and science goes beyond the superficial diagnosis that science overturns traditional religious worldviews. Nihilism is not the same as science. It is concerned with awakening "elemental subjectivity" from within the conflict between religion and science. This is the "new angle" Nishitani spoke of, from which the two are seen to converge at "the question of modern man's awareness of his own subjectivity."[44] This means that nihility can be overcome at the place where it is most nihility, at the bottom of the abyss of a Godless and meaningless existence. Moreover, this overcoming can only be accomplished by the self who appropriates the experience of nihility as part of its true self.

This is what Nishitani designates the field of emptiness: "The concept of *śūnyatā*... was born from the realization of the abyss of nihility right under the feet of every human existence."[45] It is where Nietzsche stood when he proclaimed the death of God and where science stands when it denies that the natural world has a beginning and an end. But it is also the place of religious awakening to the true self. In this field, the nihility turns into the creative field. The overcoming of nihilism by radicalizing nihilism is not a strategy devised from without. It is an essential trait of nihilism itself. Nihility can only negate nihility on the field of nihility. This affirmation through a negation of a negation is only possible on the field of *śūnyatā*, to which we turn our attention next.

"The standpoint of emptiness," Nishitani's crowning philosophical concept, took shape during his struggles to integrate his analysis of nihilism with the Buddhist idea of *śūnyatā*. The two are mutually defining. Emptiness is not a "solution" to the "problem" of nihilism but its natural outflow. And because Nishitani saw Nietzsche's nihilism as a historical and philosophical response to modern science, emptiness and nihilism need to integrate the scientific worldview into the picture. This threefold unity, as Van Bragt has noted, is a distinguishing feature of Nishitani's Buddhist philosophy.

Śūnyatā is usually translated as emptiness or nothingness. *Nothingness* and *absolute nothingness* were key concepts for the philosophers of the Kyoto School, but Nishitani came to prefer the Buddhist term *śūnyatā*.[46] This does not represent so much a difference of philosophical content as it does Nishitani's desire for a term linguistically differentiated from the Japanese translation of the European terms for nihility and atheism.[47]

In Buddhism, in especially the Mahāyāna tradition, *śūnyatā* derives from awakening to the reality of "dependent origination" (*pratītyasamutpāda*), that everything exists in mutual, "circuminsessional" relationship with everything else. Accordingly, individual things are without a stable and unchanging substance or "self-nature"(*svabhāva*).[48] Precisely because of this lack of a self-nature, things can only exist co-dependently. Nāgārjuna (ca. 150–250), who is credited with the most important Mahāyāna text on emptiness, put it this way: "We state that whatever is dependently arising, that is emptiness. That is dependent upon convention. That itself is the middle path."[49] As such, *śūnyatā* itself is no more than a provisional name for something that exists only in mutual relationships.

Nishitani often refers to "the field of emptiness" in place of "the standpoint of emptiness," suggesting a connection with the notion of a field of force in physics. Huayan Buddhism speak of *dharmadhātu*,[50] field or *topos* on which

> each individual is at once the cause for the whole and is caused by the whole, and what is called existence is a vast body made up of an infinity of individuals all sustaining each other and defining each other.[51]

How does one enter the world of *dharmadhātu* or step onto the field of emptiness? We recall that Nishitani sees the way to overcoming nihilism or atheism as going to its ground and breaking through it, which requires its radical subjectivization. In other words, authentic subjectivity takes place only in "awakening to a nihility within human nature that lies beyond the reach of reason and yet constitutes the very ground on which we stand." The true self is achieved, paradoxically, by accepting the groundlessness of the self. One has first "to feel this nihility underfoot" in order to "break through the 'existence' of things all at once, to pass beyond that dimension in which each and every thing in the world is thought to have an objective existence."[52]

But here again we have to ask: How is it possible to overcome nihilism by accepting the nihility at our feet? How can we step over nihilism when there are no stepping stone left to stand on? In his analysis of Nishitani's standpoint of emptiness, Hase points out that, on the field of emptiness, the fact of not having any stepping stone is the very stepping stone we need, "because the philosophy of emptiness is even more radical than nihilism, since there lies at its core an absolute negation that breaks through everything intrinsic to humans." He goes on:

> In emptiness, there is no place where we can place our hands and feet, no place where we can lay our heads. But complete lack of emotions and thorough disregard for personal gain, both rooted in emptiness, are said to characterize the Buddhas. This is the standpoint of emptiness. Emptiness appeared in Buddhism as something which breaks through the complete self-centeredness which is expressed in the Buddhist tradition most succinctly through the philosophy of *karma* and transmigration. Similarly, only the absolute negation of emptiness can break through the negativity and self-centeredness of nihilism from the inside. Emptiness gains its philosophical power to break through nihilism from the inside of the Buddhist tradition.[53]

In a word, "the Buddhist standpoint of emptiness is a unique way of transcendence that makes the overcoming of that nihility of nihilism possible."[54] Negating the nihility of nihilism according to the intrinsic dynamic of nihilism begins by doubting oneself as a self-enclosed subject. Nihilism offers us the opportunity to crack open the solid shell we call "self" and step out into the the standpoint of emptiness:

> What is closed in within itself can be opened only from the inside. And to open a thing from the inside becomes possible only by reaching the very own-reality of the thing. Emptiness is the path to the self-reality of thing. There then lies the reason why the overcoming of nihilism is said to be effected in emptiness. The transcendence at work in emptiness does not consist in elevating being over nothingness, life over death, meaning over meaningless.... It is the path of escape from meaninglessness and nihility by a total acceptance of nihility as nihility and meaninglessness as meaninglessness and by going deeper and deeper into nihility and meaninglessness.[55]

The standpoint of emptiness allows for the negation of negation because it denies being and, at the same time, non-being. Emptiness recognizes that even its own "standpoint" is empty, and thereby affirms it in a double negation. Emptiness is "absolute non-attachment," free of all confinement. It "empties itself even of the standpoint that represents it as some 'thing' that is emptiness." Buddhism expresses this in the cryptic formula, "Form is emptiness, emptiness is form," or in its philosophical form, "Being is nothingness, nothingness is being."[56] Emptiness discloses to us that our existence lacks its own self-enclosed ground, that everything that exists, exists only in reciprocal dependency. Standing on the field of emptiness, the self-enclosed "self" collapses into a groundless nothingness, and at the same time awakens to that groundlessness as very ground of the existence of our true self. Here again, the negation of negation is crucial: "Just as nihility is an abyss for anything that exists, emptiness may be said to be an abyss even for that abyss of nihility."[57]

Now to view the conflict between religion and science against the horizon of *śūnyatā* is to dissolve conventional modes of thought that distinguish between them as absolute and relative, spiritual and the material, personal and impersonal. Nietsche's announcement of God's death was also a declaration of the end of thinking in terms of those dichotomies. This is why Nishitani felt the need to approach things from a "new angle," where religion that has passed through nihilism can embrace the nihility of the scientific spirit into its own subjectivity. In the traditional Christian worldview, the world was created by God and sustained by a divine providence that ensured the place of human beings as the crown of creation are living in personal relationship with their creator. Modern science, however, has come to see the world as indifferent to human interests, which "has cut across the personal relationship between God and man."[58] Nishitani explains:

> The total impersonality of the world came to appear as something qualitatively different from either human or divine "personality." In effect, the world cut through the personal relationship between God and man. This means that man is no longer merely *personally* in the world. As a being who is both completely material and completely biological, he is ruled by the indifferent laws of nature. Those laws embrace everything in the world—non-living, living, and human— and govern without regard for such distinctions. Human interests make no dif-

ference, either.... These laws display in both cases the same cold inhumanity, the same indifference to human interests. Those laws still rule over everything that exists, including man.[59]

Nishitani's "new angle," then, is to incorporate the problem of religion and science into "the question of modern man's awareness of his own subjectivity."[60] As nihilism has made clear, when it comes to God, religions "have tended to put the emphasis exclusively on the aspect of life," that is, on "the personal relationship between God and man." In contrast, Buddhism locates death within life. Nishitani illustrates this with a method of meditation known as the "death's-head contemplation." Seated in front of a skull, one contemplates the fact that "from the very outset life is at one with death, ... that all living things, just as they are, can be seen under the form of death."[61] The world of death "cuts across" the world of life. Reality discloses itself to us in a "double exposure" where death is overlaid on life. The same applies to the opposition between religion and science, being and nonbeing, spirit and matter:

> This kind of double exposure is a true vision of reality. Reality itself requires it. In it, spirit, personality, life, and matter all come together and lose their separateness. They appear like the various tomographic plates of a single subject. Each plate belongs to reality, but the basic reality is the superimposition of all the plates into a single whole that admits to being represented layer by layer. It is not as if only one of the representations were true, so that all the others can be reduced to it. Reality eludes all such attempts at reduction. In the same sense, the aspect of life and the aspect of death are equally real, and reality is that which appears now as life and now as death. It is *both* life and death, and at the same time is *neither* life nor death. It is what we have to call the nonduality of life and death.... The crosscut of reality which discloses the aspect of death has heretofore been called the *material*, and that which discloses the aspect of life, the *vital*. Soul, personality, spirit, and the like have been viewed exclusively from this latter aspect of life; so has been God.[62]

For Nishitani, the dichotomy between religion and science as we know it in the modern world stems from the fact that "traditional religions spin on a life-oriented axis, while the line running from the scientific viewpoint to nihilism represents a death-oriented axis." The standpoint of *śūnyatā* not only makes the dichotomy visible, it offers a way to overcome it:

The emergence of any given thing in the Form of its true suchness can be considered as the point at which the orientation to life and the orientation to death intersect. Everything can be seen as a kind of "double exposure" of life and death, of being and nihility.... I mean instead that while life remains life to the very end, and death remains death, they both become manifest in any given thing, and therefore that the aspect of life and the aspect of death in a given thing can be superimposed in such a way that both become simultaneously visible.... This could also be called a standpoint of absolute "equality," in which personality, while continuing to be personality, would nonetheless be seen as equal to material things; and material things, while retaining their materiality, would nonetheless be seen as equal to personality. It is the very standpoint of *śūnyatā* itself that enables such a viewpoint to come about.[63]

By overlaying the viewpoints of religion and science on reality into a double exposure, the possibility that either of them can represent reality on their own is negated. Religion negates the nihilism that was brought about by the "impersonal" indifference of nature; science negates the objectification of the basis of religion in such things as an absolute and "personal" God. In other words, the dichotomy of being and non-being, personal and impersonal dissolves in the double exposure where form is seen as emptiness and emptiness as form. This is Nishitani's starting point for a creative integration of religion and science:

When we say "being-*sive*-nothingness," or "form is emptiness; emptiness is form," we do not mean that what are initially conceived of as *being* on one side and *nothingness* on the other have later been joined together. In the context of Mahāyāna thought, the primary principle of which is to transcend all duality emerging from logical analysis, the phrase "being-*sive*-nothingness" requires that one take up the stance of "*sive*" and from there view being as being and nothingness as nothingness. Ordinarily, of course, we occupy a standpoint shackled to being, from which being is viewed solely as being. Should such a standpoint be broken through and denied, nihility appears. But this standpoint of nihility in turn becomes a standpoint shackled to nothingness, from which nothingness is viewed solely as nothingness, so that it, too, needs to be negated. It is here that emptiness, as a standpoint of absolute non-attachment liberated from this double confinement, comes to the fore.[64]

From the standpoint of emptiness, the life-axis of religion intersects with the death-axis of science, the idea of ultimate reality as personal intersects with the impersonal. Life becomes the ground of death, and death the ground of life:

> But now, what would happen if we were to stick to looking at things directly, as they are in their proper Form of life-*sive*-death, death-*sive*-life? It might be that a leap would take place here, too, though it would not be a leap upward along a line of development ascending toward personality, nor a leap downward along a line of reduction descending toward materiality. Rather, it would have to take place directly underfoot of the proper Form of things as life-*sive*-death, death-*sive*-life.[65]

The mindset of life-*sive*-death and death-*sive*-life is only possible on a field of absolute equality where life is negated by death and death by life. This mutual negation requires that emptiness of the double negation does not assume the role of a transcendent, unifying absolute but empties itself:

> Emptiness in the sense of *śūnyatā* is emptiness only when it empties itself even of the standpoint that represents it as some "thing" that is emptiness. It is, in its original Form, self-emptying. In this meaning, true emptiness is not to be posited as something outside of and other than "being." Rather, it is to be realized as something united to and self-identical with being.... Ordinarily, of course, we occupy a standpoint shackled to being, from which being is viewed solely as being. Should such a standpoint be broken through and denied, nihility appears. But this standpoint of nihility in turn becomes a standpoint shackled to nothingness, from which nothingness is viewed solely as nothingness, so that it, too, needs to be negated. It is here that emptiness, as a standpoint of absolute non-attachment liberated from this double confinement, comes to the fore.[66]

Let us not lose sight of Nishitani's motivation for thinking of reality in double exposure: to overcome nihilism. The urgency of this problem is a function of the pivotal role that a personal understanding of ultimate reality had played prior to the emergence of the natural sciences in the sixteenth century. Deprived of divine providence, nature and history lost the meaning and telos to the blind and reckless laws that govern the world:

> The laws of the natural world that rule over life and matter alike that govern life as well as death are in themselves indifferent to questions of our life and death, the fortune and misfortune that comes our way, of the good and evil we do. Nature greets with indifference distinctions like these that belong to the

concerns of man. Nature's insensitivity is felt in the circle of man as distant and unfeeling, at times even as coldhearted and cruel.[67]

The divine creator who had once been the ground of nature and history was transformed into an abyss of nihility. Nishitani cites Dostoevsky's *Notes from the Underground* in support of his claim that

> within the world of nature and its scientific laws, all of which has become both indifferent to and paradoxical for human existence, we can see unfolding in our times a problem fundamental for all religions.[68]

Nishitani's description of the circuminsessional relationship between religion and science is confirmed in Whitehead's assertion that Greek tragedy and Christian faith were essential conditions for the birth of modern science in Europe and its "inexpugnable belief that every detailed occurrence can be correlated with its antecedents in a perfectly definite manner, exemplifying general principles." This belief can be traced back to

> the medieval insistence on God's rationality, conceived as with the personal energy of Jehovah and with the rationality of a Greek philosopher.... Every detail was supervised and ordered: the search into nature could only result in the vindication of the faith in rationality.

Moreover, he continues, "the pilgrim fathers of the scientific imagination as it exists today are the great tragedians of ancient Athens, Aeschylus, Sophocles, Euripides," whose vision on the fate of human beings as something "remorseless and indifferent" and "inevitable" is the very vision possessed by science. "Fate in Greek Tragedy becomes the order of nature in modern thought... The law of physics are the decree of fate."[69]

Whitehead adds one more factor to explain why modern science evolved in Europe rather than in Asia or elsewhere, namely, "a widespread instinctive conviction in the existence of an Order of Things, and, in particular, of an Order of Nature." The transformation of this instinct into an "inexpugnable belief," he concluded, is rooted in a belief in the rationality of a personal God.

For Nishitani, the standpoint of *śūnyatā* is a frame of reference within which both the idea of God as a heteronymous ruler of the cosmos and the idea of human beings as shackled by the fate of the natural world can be overthrown simultaneously. It is there that we break through the personality of

God to the impersonality of the Godhead, which is as indifferent to human existence as the laws of nature that control our fate. The impersonal God combined with the heartless dominion of nature drive us to the meaninglessness of life, but by subjectifying that nihility into an *amor fati,* a life deprived of its foundations is converted into a life free of attachment:

> For these reasons, what we have called the abyss of nihility can only be constituted in emptiness. Even for nihility to be so *represented* is possible only in emptiness. In this sense, just as nihility is an abyss for anything that exists, emptiness may be said to be an abyss even for that abyss of nihility.[70]

The death that negates life is itself negated and transformed into life. Life after the breakthrough is the same life, yet somehow not the same for having been negated and reaffirmed. In Nishitani's words, "only 0° can at the same time be 360°,"[71] and that is only possible for a subject that has been consciously engaged in the self-negation of life.

THE INDIFFERENT LOVE OF GOD AND THE INDIFFERENT LAWS OF NATURE

What has all of this to do with Christian theology's dialogue with Buddhism in an age conditioned by an uncompromising reliance on science? If we agree that faith in a personal God was instrumental in bringing natural science to its position of dominance in Christian Europe, the rejection of the idea of a personal God in nihilism through the prompting of natural science leads us to ask whether or not there might still be something worth redeeming from the idea. Insofar as belief in a personal God paved the way for science, at least indirectly it can be said to have led to its own negation and replacement with a radically impersonal view of reality. But is that the whole of it? I suggest that the problem of the personal and the impersonal is much more complicated than it seems at first glance. If we grant, with Whitehead, that belief in both a personal God and an impersonal fate were necessary for science, does the latter simply obliterate the former, or is there some wider framework within which to integrate the two?

Nishitani links the possibility of a genuine relationship between individuals to selflessness and from there argues for the impersonal character of God. One of his commentators, Suzuki Kō, explains:

The absolute is not a person. Viewing the absolute as personal derives from the medieval opposition between a first-person I and a second-person Thou that transcends the I. This is not the way of modern religious thinking. From the start, the second-person Thou that opposes the I can only be a finite relative like the I. The absolute is place that mediates the finite I and the finite Thou through self-negation.[72]

The dichotomy between the "personal" and the "impersonal" that surfaces in the conflict between religion and science is dissolved in the Buddhist worldview by relating them as interdependent, finite relatives. Given Nishitani's affection for the New Testament, it is not surprising to find him citing the Sermon on the Mount as a kind of *kōan* for reflecting on their "circum-insessional interpenetration":

> "You have heard that it was said, 'You shall love your neighbor and hate your enemy.' But I say to you, Love your enemies and pray for those who persecute you, so that you may be children of your Father in heaven; for he makes his sun rise on the evil and on the good, and sends rain on the righteous and on the unrighteous. For if you love those who love you, what reward do you have? Do not even the tax collectors do the same? And if you greet only your brothers and sisters, what more are you doing than others? Do not even the Gentiles do the same? Be perfect, therefore, as your heavenly Father is perfect. (Matt 5:43–8)

From this passage, Nishitani distinguishes two types of "indifference" in the fundamental structure of reality. The indifference of nature, which is reflected in the consistency of its operations, "reduces everything to the level of the highest abstract common denominator, be it matter or some particular physical element." In contrast, the indifferent love of God "embraces all things in their most concrete Form—for example, good men and evil men—and accepts the differences for what they are." This, says Nishitani, is the way to view the relationship between religion and science.[73] On the standpoint of emptiness, the heartless indifference of the material world is traversed by the indifferent love of God, and vice versa. They ground each other by each negating the ground of the other.

Nishitani disassociates his idea of the impersonality of God from the traditional understanding of God's omnipresence, which is experienced as the absolute negation of the being of all creatures and sets up "an iron wall that blocks all movement forward or backward." On the contrary, the image of an omnipresent God points to the impersonal character of the divine and to the abyss of nihility in everything created by such an impersonal divinity. In other words, God can be said to be omnipresent because God transcends personal being and, at the same time, deprives created beings of any ground for self-sufficiency. Inasmuch as the standpoint of emptiness is "a standpoint of absolute non-attachment,"[74] it provides a way to integrate the personal and the impersonal into our understanding of what it means to be a "person":

> We have here the possibility of a totally different way of viewing the personal, and, therefore, the impersonal. It is what we should call an "impersonally personal relationship" or a "personally impersonal relationship." The original meaning of *persona* probably comes close to what we are speaking of. In Christianity, the Holy Spirit has this characteristic. While being thought of as one *persona* of the Trinity, it is at the same time the very love of God itself, the breath of God; it is a sort of impersonal person or personal nonperson, as it were. But once such a point of view is introduced, not only the character of the Holy Spirit, but also that of God himself who contains this spirit, and of man in his "spiritual" relationship with God (as well as the character of that relationship itself), have to be seen on a new horizon.[75]

Viewing the world in "double exposure" through the lens of *śūnyatā* brings into relief both the indifference of God's love and the indifference of nature's laws. The effect is a *decentering* of the self. On one hand, awareness of the indifferent, all-embracing love of God is not acknowledgment of an objective but a confession of our own self-centerdness. We sinners receive the love of God not because of who we are but only because God "makes his sun rise on the evil and on the good, and sends rain on the righteous and on the unrighteous." The egoistic self is decentered and dispossessed of the ground of its being in when we awaken to the indifference with which God's love is extended to all things. On the other hand, the idea of a monotheistic God based on the dichotomy between "true and false" and "friend and enemy" is exposed as a self-centered view of the world. We will have more to say of this in the following chapter. Our point here is that only the decentered self is able to understand God's love at it source:

> What is it like, this non-differentiating love, this *agape*, that loves even enemies? In a world, it is "making oneself empty."... God's love is such that it

shows itself willing to forgive even the sinner who has turned against him, and this forgiving love is an expression of the "perfection" of God who embraces without distinction the evil as well as the good. Accordingly, the meaning of self-emptying may be said to be contained within God himself.[76]

The indifference of divine love contrasts with the indifference of nature, which reduces everything to matter governed by laws. If the indifference of God's love lays bare one's own sinfulness, the indifference of nature brings us to an "awareness of nihility penetrating deep beneath the world of natural laws and inhuman rationality with which science is preoccupied," and through that very awareness, "opens up a horizon that enables freedom beyond necessity and life beyond rationality."[77] Nature's indifference to human interests, as Nietzsche had said, unroots us from the center of reality and sends us spinning off towards an unknown "x."[78] The merciless forward march of natural evolution, as Pierre Baldi argued, has decentered the human being from its role as subject of the world.

The *topos* of *śūnyatā* overlays these two aspects of indifference—represented by religion and science—to reveal the world in double exposure. Awakening to the indifferent love of God has the same effect, undercutting the indifference of nature and liberating the believer from an ego-centered understanding of God. On the standpoint of emptiness, both personal and impersonal ways of viewing reality come into question. We recognize the impersonality of the indifferent love of a personal God, and at the same time, we accept the indifferent laws of nature as the place for pursuing elemental subjectivity. The abyss of nihilism is transformed into the field of subjectivity.

> For these reasons, what we have called the abyss of nihility can only be constituted in emptiness. Even for nihility to be so *represented* is possible only in emptiness. In this sense, just as nihility is an abyss for anything that exists, emptiness may be said to be an abyss even for that abyss of nihility.[79]

Standing in emptiness, the dichotomy between the field of nihility and "the fields of sensation and reason collapses, and with it, the distinction between the "infinite dispersion" of all things on the field of nihility and the belief that, ultimately, all things are "gathered together and united." The traditional philosophical concept of an absolute One was proposed as "a single center, a center that makes the world what it is." As Nishitani observes, the problem with this way of thinking is that it "leads to the positing of a One seen as mere non-differentiation." In order for the multiplicity and differentiation of the real world to be seen as meaningful, "the system of being must be seen as something that opens up *nihility* at its ground, and not merely as a system of *being*." On the field of emptiness, as the Huayan Buddhist metaphor of Indra's net[80] depicts, everything exists on its own "home-ground" and simultaneously in "circuminsessional" relation with everything else. This mutual reflection of things

> comes about only on the field of *śūnyatā*, where the being of all other things, while remaining to the very end the being that it is, is emptied out. Moreover, this means that the autonomy of this one thing is only constituted through a subordination *to* all other things. Its autonomy comes about only on a standpoint from which it makes all other things to be what they are, and in so doing is emptied of its own being.[81]

In short, insofar as religion and science are seen as overlaying perspectives on one and the same reality, each negates the claim of the other to a self-sufficient and comprehensive worldview. Religion, as "the subjectification of the atheism," negates the nihilism that was brought about by the "impersonal" indifference of nature. In turn, science negates the attempt to objectify the foundation of religion in a God or absolute "personal" being. The either/or of being and non-being, personal and impersonal, is replaced with the both/and of double exposure. Nishitani invites us to reject a monochrome view of the world as either form or emptiness, and to seek a place to stand from which we can say, "Form is emptiness, and emptiness is form."

5

A *Dhātu* of Faiths

In a self-critical mood, James Heisig looks back on decades of theological attempts at interreligious dialogue and suggests that the Christian approach suffers from a "misplaced immediacy":

> Christian theology came to be so overwhelmed by derivative debates over the nature of doctrinal truth claims in a religiously plural world that the immediacy of *contact* had been displaced by *talk about contact*. In time, it became clear to Buddhist participants that the Christians preferred to talk to themselves.[1]

Rather than allow other religious traditions to structure the dialogue from their own perspective, Heisig explains, Christian intellectuals have tended to concentrate on soliciting and evaluating the response of other religions to issues central to the Christian faith and finding the right place to locate the dialogues in their own self-understanding. I would like to take this as a starting point for the final step of my argument.

DECONSTRUCTING THE CHRISTIAN CONSTRUCTION OF RELIGIOUS PLURALISM

The monotheist construction of religious pluralism

Ever since Alan Race's classification of theological approaches to other religions into exclusivism, inclusivism, and pluralism, theologians, almost without exception, have taken up the theology of religions on the naive assumption that other religions simply "exist *alongside* the Christian faith." Accordingly, when they enter into dialogue with another religion, they see their task as replying to questions that arise from "the encounter *between* Christianity and the other faith."[2] Rather than engage another faith immediately, they approach it as something that lies outside the Christian tradition and can be encountered only indirectly, through theological reflection on it.

This final chapter aims to take a critical look at the soil in which such thinking took root. It seeks what Whitehead called the basic "form of the forms of thought":

> When you are criticizing the philosophy of an epoch, do not chiefly direct your attention to those intellectual positions which its exponents feel it necessary explicitly to defend. There will be some fundamental assumptions which adherents of all the variant systems within the epoch unconsciously presuppose. Such assumptions appear so obvious that people do not know what they are assuming because no other way of putting this has ever occurred to them. With these assumptions a certain limited number of types of philosophic systems are possible, and this group of systems constitutes the philosophy of the epoch.[3]

To lay out the fundamental assumption that shapes the way Christian theology approaches other traditions in their concrete reality, we may return to Troeltsch. I agree with Knitter that, "Much of what we feel concerning religious pluralism is mirrored in Ernst Troeltsch,"[4] including Race's models of exclusivism, inclusivism, and pluralism. But the one underlying assumption that all these approaches share is captured succinctly in his lecture on the place of Christianity among world religions: "In our earthly experience, the Divine Life is not one, but many. However, to apprehend the one in the many constitutes the special character of love."[5] As noble as this sentiment is, the unquestioning commitment to the ultimate oneness of the truth is also a source of aggression and violence toward other religions.

It may seem absurd to associate theologies of religious pluralism with violence, given that their purpose was precisely to counter the psychological and physical conflicts that have stained relations among religious traditions throughout history. Are theologies of religious pluralism not an effort to overcome Christian exclusivism?

The rejoinder is not without merit. In an earlier chapter, we saw how the endeavor to steer theology toward the reality of a religiously plural world grew out of a critical reappraisal of traditional approaches whose arrogance had led to misunderstanding and intolerance towards "non-Christian" faiths.

As Jeffrey Haynes observes, up to the present "many current international conflicts have religious aspects that can exacerbate both hatred and violence and make the conflicts themselves exceptionally difficult to resolve."[6] He cites Hans Küng in this regard:

> The most fanatical, the cruelest political struggles are those that have been colored, inspired, and legitimized by religion. To say this is not to reduce all political conflicts to religious ones, but to take seriously the fact that religions share in the responsibility for bringing peace to our torn and warring world.[7]

If religious exclusivism spawns violence—psychological, mental, physical, or political—and the acknowledgment of religious pluralism militates against exclusivism, a theology of religious pluralism would seem to be immune from criticism. But matters are not so simple. Two questions require closer attention:

1. What is the source of the exclusivist posture of the Christian faith toward other religions?
2. Is the theology of religious pluralism, at least in its current form and content, really free of exclusivism or is it just a contemporary variant?

The fundamental assumption on which theologians by and large rely in their reflections on other religions comes down to this: There is *one and only one truth*, which is revealed in and through the Christian faith. Interreligious dialogue and religious pluralism are of interest insofar as they are concerned with that truth and express in a different form. In what follows, I propose to argue that so-called "inclusivist" and "pluralist" approaches rest on the same assumption of *one and only one truth*. In this sense, they are fruits of the same tree as exclusivism.

The Christian framework in which other religions are interpreted and evaluated is defined by a commitment to a single, ultimate truth. We may call this a "theological semantics," similar to the "cultural semantics" of which Jan Assmann, the eminent German Egyptologist, speaks. The distinctive modes of behavior and thought that belong to a particular worldview follow "a semantic paradigm expressed in grand stories and differentiation"[8] and transmitted as "cultural memory."[9] What is essential in a cultural semantics is not the historical fact, but the "collective memory" that shapes and sustains the identity of a given culture or a society.

For Assmann, the cultural semantics of the monotheistic religions is governed by the belief that "there is no God but one," and "no idol in the world really exists" (1 Cor 8:4). If there can be only one God, it is logical to conclude that anything else called "God" should either be set aside as false or absorbed into the true God. As a result, the theological semantics of a monotheistic religion defines the logic of the existential question about God in terms of a choice between "true or false," which in turn is adopted in the political sphere to discern between "friends and enemies."

Assmann adopts the term "the political" (*das Politische*) as a way to distinguish between friends and enemies from the Nazi ideologist Carl Schmitt (1888–1985),[10] who was influenced by his own experience growing up among the Catholic minority in Protestant Prussia.[11] Similarly, when the Harvard political scientist Samuel Huntington sounded the alarm against large-scale immigration into the United States, he appealed to the logic of exclusivism as a way of cementing group identity: "'You' and 'I' become 'we' when 'they' appears."[12] Traces of an exclusivist understanding of identity are also evident throughout the Old Testament in accounts of the Exodus, the Ten Commandments, the covenant with God and formation of Israel, the countless wars against idolaters, and the ruthless slaughter of those who threatened that identity. Hence, Assmann argues, the cultural semantics that governs the dichotomy between friend and foe in monotheism is engraved as "the basis of our tradition and our spiritual world" in the book of Deuteronomy, which is "an absolutely central and fundamental text for both Jewish and Christian culture."[13]

As for the driving force of monotheism's "cultural semantics," Assmann agrees with Othmar Keel in pointing to the image of a jealous God. Out of jealousy, God demands "dissociation from and exclusion of other gods."[14] The memory of a "jealous God" (e.g., Exodus 20:5)—what Assmann refers to as "the Mosaic distinction"—is transferred seamlessly from the Old Testament to New, where we are enjoined to reject all "so-called gods" in favor of the one "from whom are all things and for whom we exist" (1 Cor 8:6). The God of Christian monotheism is a jealous lover who alone determines what is true and what is false in religion:

The distinction I am concerned with in this book is the distinction between true and false in religion that underlies more specific distinctions such as Jews and Gentiles, Christians and pagans, Muslims and unbelievers. Once the distinction is drawn, there is no end of reentries or subdistinctions. We start with Christians and pagans and end up with Catholics and Protestants, Calvinists and Lutherans, Socinians, and Latitudinarians, and a thousand more similar denominations and subdenominations. Cultural or intellectual distinctions such as these construct a universe that is not only full of meaning, identity, and orientation, but also full of conflict, intolerance, and violence. Therefore, there have always been attempts to overcome the conflict by reexamining the distinction, albeit at the risk of losing cultural meaning. Let us call the distinction between true and false in religion the "Mosaic distinction" because tradition ascribes it to Moses.... Moses is a figure of memory but not of history, while Akhenaten is a figure of history but not of memory. Since memory is all that counts in the sphere of cultural distinctions and constructions, we are justified in speaking not of Akhenaten's distinction, but of the Mosaic distinction. The space severed or cloven by this distinction is the space of Western monotheism. It is this constructed mental or cultural space that has been inhabited by Europeans for nearly two millennia.[15]

For Assmann, the Mosaic distinction amounted to "a revolutionary counter-religion" that was accompanied by "the construction of antagonistic conceptions such as 'paganism' or 'idolatry.'"[16] To a consciousness shaped by the images and beliefs of monotheism, polytheism is stripped of its spiritual meaning and discarded as a "religious error."[17]

The Mosaic distinction refers, as I have already mentioned, to the distinction between true and false religion. My thesis is that this distinction represents a revolutionary innovation in the history of religion. It was unknown to traditional, historically evolved religions and cultures. Here the key differences were those between the sacred and the profane or the pure and the impure. Neglecting an important deity amounted to a far more serious offense than worshipping false gods, the chief concern of secondary religions. In principle, all religions had the same truth-value and it was generally acknowledged that relations of translatability pertained between foreign gods and one's own. The transition from primary to secondary religious experience therefore goes hand in hand with a new construction of identity and alterity that blocks such translatability. In place of what one could call a "hermeneutics of translation," there now appears a "hermeneutics of difference," which assures itself of what is its own by staking its distance from the Other, proceeding in accordance with the principle *"Omnis determinatio est negatio."*[18]

Paradoxically, it is not monotheism but polytheism that best helps distinguish one religion from another. In polytheism "each deity stands for a distinction" and "each people, tribe, and city has its own tutelary deity and finds expression for its differentiated identity in a correspondingly differentiated divine world." In contrast, "monotheism is the religion not of distinctions but of unity and universalism." But it is just this unity and universalism that turns it to violence. Like the jealous God who demands exclusivity, monotheism's way of loving other religions is to destroy them. "Monotheism cancels and revokes all such distinctions. Before the One God, all people are equal. Far from erecting barriers between people, monotheism tears them down."[19]

It would be a mistake to read Assmann's critique of monotheism as a plea to return to some ancient form of polytheism. Ulrich Beck's response to Assmann with a call for "subjective polytheism" is more to the point:

> The God of one's own choosing—and this is my contention—has ceased to be the one-and-only God who holds the key to salvation by assuming control over history and empowering its agents to practise intolerance and the use of force. The principle of religious hybridity helps to bring into focus the humane principle of a subjective polytheism that must not be confused with the polytheism of antiquity, nor with the facility with which missionary Christianity, for example, has proved able to integrate local religious traditions and rituals. Such individualized forms of a hybrid religiosity that transcends the boundaries of particular religions benefit not least because they act as a kind of resistance to the institutional insistence upon absolute conformity by its members.[20]

Beck's remarks remind us of Peter Berger's sociological diagnosis of the modern religiosity as a deliberate choice for one religion among many. Fittingly, the Greek root of the word *heresy*, αἵρεσις, literally means a selection from among available options, which is literally what being a Christian means today.[21] As Berger argues in his provocative book *The Heretical Imperative*, orthodoxy requires that we accept the imperative to be heretical as authentically religious. *Homo homini haereticus*—this is our reality in an age of religious pluralism. That heretical imperative invalidates the traditional assertion that Christianity is the one and only way to true salvation. To have faith in one religion no longer requires that we repudiate all others in order to follow our chosen path.

Violence in the shadow of "oneness"

In a roundabout way, the line Assmann draws between the jealous God and the narcissistic impulse of monotheistic religion to prevail over all other religions as "false" can be said to reflect our general human anxiety before death as the "absolute other" of our existence and our desire to secure "psychological mastery" over our condition through "the effort to deny death."[22] Mark Taylor makes this connection in a deconstructive strategy that aims to subvert the "logocentrism" with which Western Christian theology has tried to hold death at bay. In the face of death as an absolutely invincible other that annihilates the self eternally, one compensates by seeking the satisfaction of destroying one's relative others in the real world. This "psychology of mastery" wears the mask of Narcissus, for whom the entire world becomes a mirror in which he sees his own face reflected."[23]

Taylor sees the effort to possess the other is an indirect attempt to be in possession of oneself:

> The effort to possess the other represents an indirect attempt to possess one's own self. As the foregoing argument implies, one who struggles for self-possession relates to otherness in two seemingly contradictory ways. On the one hand, the subject is attracted to the other and thus seeks identification and/or incorporation. On the other hand, the agent is repulsed by the other and hence attempts to negate or exclude difference. Within these two rhythms lurk the contrasting forces whose paradoxical union gives birth to Narcissus: *Eros* and *Thanatos*.
>
> Aggression is the death instinct turned outward. Through this extroversion, the death drive inverts itself and becomes the denial of death. The aggressive subject attempts to preserve its integrity by negating the other, whose presence portends dispossession. Self-assertion, which aims at securing self-identity, is mediated by the domination or even the destruction of the other. Violence, however, is inextricably related to eros. Thanatos no more can be separated from eros than eros can be torn from thanatos. Successful aggression not only masters but actually consumes the other. While initially intended to be an act of exclusion, aggression entails both identification and incorporation.[24]

If aggression as violence "entails identification and incorporation," it manifests a desire to assimilate the other—in some sense, even to *love* it. To examine whether Taylor's "psychology of mastery" is in fact at work in theological approaches to other religions, let us look briefly at three representative thinkers. The first passage is from Ernst Troeltsch, who provided theology with its first clear paradigm for dealing with other religions. It is followed by quotations from John Hick and Paul Knitter:

Ernst Troeltsch
And, as all religion has thus a common goal in the Unknown, the Future, perchance in the Beyond, so too it has a common ground in the Divine Spirit ever pressing the finite mind onward towards further light and fuller consciousness, a Spirit which indwells the finite spirit, and whose ultimate union with it is the purpose of the whole many-sided process.... In our earthly experience, the Divine Life is not one, but many. However, to apprehend the one in the many constitutes the special character of love.[25]

John Hick
The great world faiths embody different perceptions and conceptions of, and correspondingly different responses to, the Real from within the major variant ways of being human.... One then sees the great world religions as different human responses to the one divine Reality, embodying different perceptions which have been formed in different historical and cultural circumstances.... Within each of them the transformation of human existence from self-centeredness to Reality-centeredness is taking place. These traditions are accordingly to be regarded as alternative soteriological "spaces" within which, or "ways" along which, men and women can find salvation/liberation/ultimate fulfillment.[26]

Paul Knitter
The many are called to be one. But it is a one that does not devour the many. The many become one precisely by remaining the many, and the one is brought about by each of the many making its distinct contribution to the others and thus to the whole.... So there is a movement not toward absolute or monistic oneness but toward what may be called "unitive pluralism": plurality constituting unity.[27]

The first quotation is from Troeltsch's posthumous manuscript, "The Place of Christianity among World Religions," which we dealt with extensively in Chapter 2. The second is a summary of what Hick calls the "pluralist hypothesis" or "Reality-centered pluralism." The third is from Knitter's description of "unitive pluralism."

To bridge the gap between historical relativism and the ideological-dogmatic absoluteness of Christianity, Troeltsch had to turn in the end to the mystical tradition, which historically had subsumed "manyness" into an ultimate "oneness" with the divine. This is a clear precedent for what we see in Hick and Knitter.

Knitter's concept of "plurality constituting unity" implies that the idea of a plurality of religions supposes an idea of "the whole." His holistic perspective is apparent in his application of the traditional model of the One and the many to the problem of religious pluralism. The question, as he himself realized, is whether it is possible to arrive at a standpoint from which to observe "the whole"? Knitter accepts the possibility that his "unitive pluralism" might be seen as a form of religious "imperialism" which holds "that there is one religion that has the power of purifying and then absorbing all the others."[28] He prefers to see Christianity and other religions as in "movement toward" a unity that protects the "plurality constituting unity."[29] Not unlike Troeltsch, he has recourse to the mystical tradition with its emphasis on an ultimate oneness "that has the power to purify and then absorb all the others."

Hick's "pluralistic hypothesis" sees different religions as different responses to the same transcendent fact: "Infinite Reality, in itself beyond the scope of other than purely formal concepts, is differently conceived, experienced and responded to from within the different cultural ways of being human.[30] In his critique, Mark Heim argues that "Hick fails to specify a possible future state of affairs predicted by his hypothesis that is distinguishable from concrete religious fulfillments envisioned by the traditions." In short, the argument fails because it is possible for us to attain the "God's-eye view" we would need to verify it.[31]

Heim's suspicions are not unfounded. As Hick acknowledges in an imaginary dialogue with a philosopher named Phil that the historical roots of religious pluralism can be traced back to the "European Enlightenment of the seventeenth and eighteenth centuries with its universalizing rationalism," a time when "Westerners first began to think on a world scale and to consider religion generically, seeing the particular historical religions as its different forms." He goes on:

> Kant, for example, held that there is only one (true) religion; but there can be faiths [i.e., creeds or "ecclesiastical faiths"] of several kinds. That is the background. Now contemporary religious pluralism had arisen after the Second World War when the European colonial hegemony finally ended and when a general awareness came about, at least in the West, of the world as a single interdependent unity, with the image of "one world" and "the global village" becoming common.[32]

Hick admits that viewing religious pluralism as a "child of the European Enlightenment" in search of a universal unity of religions supports the criticism "that religious pluralism ignores or dismisses the concrete differences between the traditions, homogenizing them into a false unity." Postmodern thinkers in particular tend to dismiss religious pluralism as an "all totalizing thinking" with "a global meta-narrative that subordinates all individual and communal narratives, thus undermining 'alterity' and eliminating the otherness of the Other."[33] As a result, all forms of "unitive pluralism" have to contend with the temptation to an ideological imperialism that endeavors to fold all religions into a single faith, namely, Christianity.

The operative model for all three—Troeltsch, Hick, and Knitter—is the unity of the One and the many. Not surprisingly, the "One" refers to something absolute, transcendental, and ultimate, while the "many" points to what is relative, immanent, and temporal. This way of setting up the problem is familiar to Western theology, where "being is interpreted in terms of oneness and presence. To be is to be one, and to be one is, in some sense, to be uniquely and irreducibly present."[34] In other words, *to be oneself* means *not to be the other* or lose oneself in the other:

> From a monotheistic perspective, to be is to be one. In order to be one, the subject cannot err and must always remain proper. By following the straight and narrow course, the self hopes to gain its most precious possession-itself.... The interplay of oneness and ownness implies the inextricable relation between propriety and proximity.[35]

The disposition toward "oneness" is intrinsically violent, in the sense that it tends to exclude the reality of the other. Just as the relative *one* establishes its identity by excluding the other from itself, so, too, the absolute *One* erases the real differences among relative others by absorbing them into itself. The *one* is reflected in the *One* and vice versa.

THE *ADVAITIC* PLURALISM OF RAIMON PANIKKAR

As noted earlier, in discussions of religious pluralism, oneness has sometimes referred to the absoluteness of the Christian faith which is to be defended by all means against the plurality of religions. At other times, oneness has taken on a more inclusive meaning that allows Christianity to acknowledge the varieties of religious truth. Finally, oneness has been taken to hypothesize a common ground for all the religions beyond their cultural and historical differences. In each case, the concept of oneness does violence to other religions. Might there be some other way to liberate the theology of religious pluralism from its violent tendencies? Where might we look for a paradigm shift from one-centeredness to many-centeredness?

The main problem, of course, is getting over our fixation on oneness. The writings of the Catalan philosopher and theologian, Raimon Panikkar, is an invaluable resource here. As one of his commentators has remarked, Panikkar is one of those few extraordinary thinkers who already live in the so-called "Second Axial Period,"[36] acutely conscious of the religious traditions of Asia active within his personal faith. He describes the spiritual journey that brought him from Europe to Asia and back again in a simple formula: "I 'left' as a Christian, I 'found' myself a Hindu, and I 'return' a Buddhist, without having ceased to be a Christian."[37] The overriding struggle of his life has been to answer the question of "whether such an attitude is objectively tenable or even intelligible."[38] It begins with clarifying "what it means today to be a Christian," which in turn leads him to ask, "Does one need to be spiritually a Semite or intellectually a Westerner in order to be a Christian?"[39] In response, Panikkar uses the metaphor of three rivers, the Jordan, the Tiber, and the Ganges," each representing what he calls a "kairological moment for Christic self-consciousness."

Panikkar was born in northern Spain of a Catalan mother and an upper-caste Indian father. In his own words, he was raised "in a double tradition— Catholic, and Hindu—and later was absorbed by Buddhism." The plural religious traditions that underlie Panikkar's spirituality explain what one commentator has called "his golden rule of hermeneutics: that we describe the other in such a manner as he can recognize himself in that description."[40] They also witness to his desire "to speak a language that will make sense for the follower of more than one philosophical tradition."[41] The enormity of the task he set himself arose from cross-cultural and interreligious investigations into the foundations of his Christian faith. At no point did he claim the possibility—or even the desirability—of a universal, objective standpoint from which to understand other religious traditions. On the contrary, his hermeneutics demand an unending search for understanding from within the particularity of one's own faith.

Panikkar's connection to other religions is not external; they reside within his Christian faith, where he is able to "pass over" from one belief to another. For this reason, Knitter characterizes him as a "radical pluralist."[42] He is "pluralist" because his search for the meaning of ultimate reality involves dialogue with other religious traditions. And he is "radical" because dialogue reaches deep into the roots of his own and other faiths. In passing over from Christianity to Asian religions and back again, it is not only that Hinduism and Buddhism became a *hermeneutical* horizon for the understanding of Christian reality, but also a *spiritual* basis for his Christian faith.

Panikkar's approach to religious pluralism differs markedly from theologians like John Hick who interpret the world's religious traditions as different paths to the ultimate unity. Panikkar is dissatisfied with this form of pluralism because of its "universalizing syndrome"[43] and the "anonymous imperialism" of its view of Christianity. Authentic religious pluralism is not a theoretical or metaphysical search for unity but a "problem of the other."[44] It is not mere numerical "plurality or reduction of plurality to unity." It does not consider unity "an indispensable ideal, even if allowance is made for variations within that unity." In effect,

> pluralism affirms neither that the truth is one nor that it is many. Rather, pluralism adopts a non-dualistic, *advaitic* attitude. It is a standpoint that is incommensurable with either unity or plurality. Pluralism, which does not permit a "universal system," in effect, "expresses an attitude of cosmic confidence (in the Spirit, which is not subordinate to the logos), which allows for a polar and tensile coexistence between *ultimate* human attitudes, cosmologies, and religions...."

The Christian pluralist will not affirm that there are many saviors. This is a nonpluralistic assertion. The pluralistic Christological affirmation will begin—as with the Trinity (*Qui incipit numerare incipit errare* [Who begins to count, begins to err], said Augustine)—by denying the meaningfulness of any quantitative individualization in the Mystery of Christ. The saving power—which is Christian and all Christ—is neither one nor many.[45]

In his essay on the three rivers alluded to above, the rivers Jordan, Tiber, and Ganges symbolize a different form of pluralism. The Ganges, which transcends the spirituality of the Jordan and the theology of the Tiber, represents "a special awareness of the other(s) and a certain inclination to welcome without suffocating them—that is, to accept without comprehending" religious traditions that are in themselves "incommensurable." It is impossible to measure all religious traditions adequately with the same *metron*. Panikkar calls instead for "a healthy pluralism... that in no way dilutes the particular contribution of each human tradition."[46] What makes it healthy is that it is "non-dualistic."[47]

As we argued in the opening chapter, religious pluralism obliges theology to ask after the way it questions other religions. Instead of asking after the place of Christian faith among world religions, like Troeltsch and his followers in the West, we need to ask about the place of other religions in the Christian faith. In Panikkar's case, awakening to religious pluralism in Asia as an inner otherness disqualifies all forms of "monocentric" consciousnes, or what postmodernists refer to as "logocentrism." The idea of inner otherness also erases the boundary between inner and outer. Various religious traditions flow into the Christian faith like the streams that come together in the Ganges River:

> The Ganges has many sources, among them one that is invisible. The Ganges disappears in a delta of countless river beds, and the Ganges has witnessed the birth of many religions along its banks.... The person rooted in such mentalities finds little meaning in common Christian theology.... Whatever the "essence" of religion may be, living and real religions are not essences but concrete, powerful, and dangerous existences. Religious rivers are much more than the H_2O of chemistry.[48]

The metaphor of faith as a flowing river has consequences not only for the self-consciousness of religious pluralism but also for the way we look at interreligious dialogue. First of all, faith is an organic phenomenon. The heteronymous traditions that come together in faith cannot be separated from each other and still belong to faith. Earlier we referred to the intrinsically plural identity found in Asian religious traditions and to the fact that the history of religions in Asia is embodied in the living faith of Asian Christians. Thomas Kasulis explains the process with reference to the "assimilation theory of truth":

> Perhaps we need to coin a new term capturing the theory of truth involved in an intimacy orientation. In this book we will call it the "assimilation theory of truth."... The term "assimilation" is used in physiology to indicate the process by which the body takes in nutrients from the food that has been ingested and digested. From the standpoint of intimacy, knowledge is absorbed into the body somatically through praxis. Knowledge is literally incorporated rather than received from outside or generated from inside.... In an important sense, intimate knowledge is not something the person has. Instead it is what that person, at least in part, is. (In Sanskrit, *satya* means both "being" and "truth.") Knowledge is assimilated, not acquired. It resides in the overlap between the knower and the known.[49]

Kasulis distinguishes "intimacy knowledge" from "integrity knowledge." Integrity knowledge is based on "publicly verifiable objectivity," which requires the knower to assume the posture of an observer at a distance from the known. In principle, this integrity relationship can be broken at any time when the connection of the knower to the known is no longer of any use. In the case of intimacy knowledge, however, the known cannot be separated from the knower because the former has "somatically" become an indispensable part of the knower. When the knower is distanced from the known by force, both undergo a fatal injury. Part of the knower is lost when the known is taken away.

The idea of intimacy knowledge as somatically assimilated by the knower is useful for grasping the relationship between the history of religions in Asia and the Christians who inherit that history today. Their knowledge of other religions is not *about* something that exists apart from them, "out there" as it were, but has been *incorporated* into their Christian faith. In the terminology of Huayan Buddhist philosophy, the connections is one of simultaneity, interdependence, and interpenetration.

Faith is an organic and syncretic phenomenon; it is neither exclusive nor inclusive but essentially pluralistic. Panikkar refers to this form of Christian religious consciousness as "Christianness" to distinguish it from institutional "Christendom" as well as from the doctrinal tradition of "Christianity." What he means by this is a personal, religiously open approach to ultimate reality in the name of Christ. Once again, the Ganges River provides a concrete example of what he has in mind:

> It is certain that many former or "fallen Christians," who came during the sixties and seventies to Varanasi at the Ganges as "converted" Hindus, attained after their return home in the eighties a new Christian identity.[50]

Secondly, Panikkar's river metaphor recommends a pluralistic understanding of interreligious dialogue and of religious pluralism itself. In contrast to the kind of "unitive pluralism" grounded in the logic of the One and the many, he opts for a "nondualistic" position. The reality of religious pluralism as it is lived cannot be reduced to a theoretical or metaphysical search for oneness. It has to do with one's disposition towards what is other, not towards an ideal of unity in which the otherness of the other is absorbed or minimized. In practice, "pluralism affirms neither that the truth is one nor that it is many." Far from a "universal system" of thought, it expresses "an attitude of cosmic confidence (in the Spirit, which is not subordinate to the logos), which allows for a polar and tensile coexistence between *ultimate* human attitude, cosmologies, and religions."[51]

THE *DHĀTU* OF MANY FAITHS

In a short paper entitled "Buddhism and Pluralism," Kimura Kiyotaka, an established scholar of Japanese Buddhism, set out to explain into "the relation between Buddhism and monism or pluralism."[52] To do so, he divided the transmission of Buddhist ideas about the nature of reality into three stages: a naive pluralistic standpoint, a nihilistic monism, and a standpoint that transcends both.

The nature of Buddhist awakening or enlightenment is expressed in two teachings about *pratītyasamutpāda* (dependent origination). The first is the doctrine of the twelvefold chain of causes (*nidānas*), which holds that all suffering (*duḥkha*) in the world is caused by ignorance (*avidyā*). Second is the doctrine of the five aggregates (*skandhas*), which says that a human being is constituted by the five factors of form, sensation, perception, mental formations, and consciousness, all of which were originally thought to be substances (*asti*) in the external world.

Kimura classifies these ideas as "evidently a sort of pluralism." An essential element of Buddhist philosophy is that everything in the world has more than two causes, that there is no one thing out of which everything comes to be. The twelvefold causal chain manifests an organic transition in existence from ignorance to awakening, not a return to a primordial oneness:

> Buddhism does not give any importance to the idea of a root principle or first cause like other systems of philosophy.... According to Buddhism, human beings and all living things are self-created or self-creating. The universe is not anthropocentric; it is the co-creation of all beings. Buddhism does not believe that all things came from one cause, but that everything is invariably created out of more than two causes.[53]

The naive pluralism of this "theory of everything" (*sarvāstivāda*) was strongly criticized by Mahāyāna Buddhism, which replaced it with the idea of emptiness (*śūnyatā*) developed by Nāgārjuna and the Madhyamaka school. The standpoint of emptiness denied permanent substance to the self and all things (*dharma*) in the world. Moreover, inasmuch as *śūnyatā* itself lacks substance, there was no question of sliding back into monism. Rather, *śūnyatā* is regarded as a provisional name for that which exists only in mutual relationships. The inherently negative bent of the Madhyamaka school, Kimura maintains, promoted the fall into nihilism. To counter these tendencies, the Yogācāra school arose to teaching a monism centered on consciousness. For Yogācāra thinkers, all phenomena emerge from consciousness and it is only in consciousness that they can be said to converge. They were succeeded by the Tathāgatagarbha school, which held to the inherent identity of the Buddha with all sentient beings in virtue of a common Buddha-nature (*buddhadhātu* or *tathāgatagarbha*). This approach, too, results in monism.

Buddhist philosophy reached its highest stage of development, according to Kimura, in the view that there is no identifiable ground beyond or beneath all things, that just as they are, all things that exist, whether individually or taken together, manifest ultimate truth. As examples of this position, Kimura lists the Tiantai, Zen, and Huayan schools. Tiantai philosophy holds that all phenomena reflect the truth,[54] and Zen that the mind of sentient beings is none other than the Buddha.[55]

The Huayan school presents a more radical viewpoint. It sees our world (*lokadhātu*) as a realm constituted of the interdependence of all *dharma* (things), that is, as a *dharmadhātu* or phenomenal realm.[56] Our world, just as it is, is the Lotus Treasury World (*Padma-garbha-loka-dhatu*),[57] the world of faith and the "simultaneous interpenetrative harmonization"[58] of the phenomenal and transcendental realms. As Heinrich Dumoulin once wrote, it is in this Huayan worldview that "the cosmotheistic worldview of East Asian peoples" is most intensely realized and earnestly practiced.[59] As the most sophisticated system of thought in Mahāyāna Buddhism, the Huayan tradition may be said to present Asian Christians with a comprehensive viewpoint from which to understand and express their Christian faith in its native religious surroundings.

The Huayan school distinguishes about four *dharmadhātu*: the phenomenal realm (of things), the noumenal realm (of principle), the realm of the non-obstruction of things and principles, and the realm of non-obstruction among phenomena. This final realm represents the highest stage in the journey through reality, namely, an awakening to the intrinsic interdependence of all things. The *Avataṃsaka sūtra* describes it in terms that suggest an interdependent totality of All in One, One in All. It imagine the cosmos as "one bright pearl," the holy and universal Buddhahood of all reality:

> In each dust-mote of these worlds
> Are countless worlds and Buddhas.
> From the tip of each hair of Buddha's body
> Are revealed the indescribable Pure Lands.
> The indescribable infinite Lands
> All ensemble in a hair's tip [of Buddha].[60]

Kimura concludes his account of Buddhism's historical ascent to radical pluralism by observing:

> We need to recognize the complexity and diversity not only of Buddhism but of religions in general, and at the same time abandon the idea of establishing some

principle to ground this complexity and diversity. As Nāgārjuna and Zhuangzi argued, if you set up one such principle, it will induce rivalry and prejudice to set up others.... What we need is a way to transcend monism, dualism, and even pluralism—all at the same time.[61]

In spite of his insistence that pluralism, too, needs to be transcended, there is little doubt that Kimura favors Huayan's pluralistic approach over the "eternalism" of early Buddhism's naive pluralism and the "annihilationism" of the Madhyamaka school's rather nihilistic monism.[62]

Now how might a Huayan Buddhist understanding of ultimate reality inform the way Asian Christians see their faith with reference to the other religious traditions that have shaped their culture and spirituality throughout history? Leaving aside the full complexities of Huayan metaphysics, we may take up the basic idea of the *dharmadhātu*—or *topos*—in which "each individual is at once the cause for the whole and is caused by the whole, and what is called existence is a vast body made up of an infinity of individuals all sustaining each other and defining each other."[63] Because identity is defined in terms of total intercausality, "there is no center, or perhaps if there is one, it is everywhere."[64] Such a vision of reality not only eliminates "the fiction of a sole causal agent,"[65] it sees all "religious truth as spread out in the organic co-relational network."[66] Francis Cook writes:

> The point to the doctrine of interdependence is that things exist *only* in interdependence, for things do not exist in their own right. In Buddhism, this manner of existence is called "emptiness" (Sanskrit *śūnyatā*). Buddhism says that things are empty in the sense that they are absolutely lacking in a self-essence (*svabhāva*) by virtue of which things would have an independent existence. In reality, their existence derives strictly from interdependence.[67]

In the same way that Kimura saw the Huayan position as a synthesis of naive pluralism and the nihilistic monism, Cook cites the Japanese Buddhist Gyōnen (1240–1321) to the effect that "Fa-Tsang and Nāgārjuna accomplished the same end: both demonstrate that things do not exist independently of each other,"[68] including the absolute and the relative. The position of Fa-tsang, an influential seventh-century Chinese Huayan thinker, is that what is called *nirvāṇa*, emptiness, or Buddha nature "comes to exist in both a pure and impure form as conditional phenomena."[69]

Once the ideas of absolute and relative are seen as mutually dependent, it is a short step to argue that anything can be seen as the whole and at the same time as nothing. This is the point of Fa-Tsang's image of ten coins as an analogy for the totality of existence:

> According to the reasoning of the Huayan masters, coin two is not a self-existent entity in its context of the ten (whole). It is coin two as a result of coin one, and looked at from the standpoint of coin one, coin one is the cause and coin two is the result, i.e., it is a conditioned coin two.... Consequently, coin one exists- i.e., is a phenomenal object—and coin two is empty—i.e., exists only in a conditioned manner.... The coins are identical in their simultaneous possession of the natures of emptiness and existence.... The emptiness and existence which serve as the source for the identity of this function primarily as a means of indicating the flow of causal efficacy between a dharma considered to be cause and the totality of remaining dharma which are in this context considered to be result.[70]

For Cook, the analogy is not only metaphysical but an existential and ethical ideal for the enlightened individuals or bodhisattvas:

> Not only is the reality of identity and interdependence the basis for Bodhisattva activity, but it also acts as a moral imperative, leaving the truly moral being with no option but to act in accordance with this reality.[71]

To return to our main line of argument, what would be the result if we were "somatically" to assimilate the Huayan Buddhist understanding of reality into the self-understanding of Christian faith? To begin with, it would bind the identity of Asian Christians to the awareness that the foundations of their faith have been and continues to be shaped by its coexistence and interaction with other religions. Moreover, it would awaken them to the fact that their identity as Christians is not something whose form that can be fixed or regulated by rational reflection or institutional decree, but is always "in the making." In other words, once it is understood that their faith interpenetrates other worlds of faith, it is liberated from attachment to the objects of their own faith.

Thomas Kasulis parallels the Huayan understanding of the interdependent self in his discussion of "intimacy's view of the self," which logically culminates in the Buddhist denial of naive attachment to the "I" as an independent entity:

> In the Buddhist self's diagrammatic representation, there is no unshaded or independent part of *a* left. This lack of the independent ego—the lack of an unshaded part of *a*—is what Buddhism call *anātman*, "no ego" or "no-I." This does not mean that I am without identity; there is still the unique overlap of interdependent process defining who I am (as represented by the full circle of *a*). The major point for Buddhism, however, is that the overlaps defining *a* are completely interdependent (completely shaded) and without any trace of independent substantiality—without any untouched nucleus.[72]

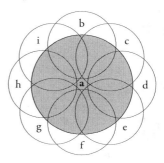

The Buddhist Self

In the Huayan Buddhist worldview, "the lack of an independent ego" is the starting point for awakening to the fullness of reality. In its Christian adaptation, this entails detachment from the position of a self-enclosed subject of faith who refuses to acknowledge its "simultaneous interpenetrative harmonization" with religious tradition different from one's own.

Among poetic expressions of the fundamental Buddhist teachings of "emptiness" and "dependent origination" we find the image of Indra's net, a vast web of clear jewels, each of which reflects the whole perfectly. Francis Cook notes its connection to the Indian concept of emptiness and "Indian Buddhism's rather general concern with causation."[73] Each individual jewel is able to stand in an unlimited and unobstructed relationship to all other jewels because it is intrinsically empty (*śūnya*) and without a nature of its own (*svabhāva*). This world of "simultaneous mutual identity and mutual intercausality" is not only an objective description of things but also of the enlightenment of the subject. As stated in the *Avataṃsaka sūtra*, the reality of the external world is reflection of the interior reality of mind:

> Just as the magicians' art
> Can make various things appear
> Due to the force of beings' acts

> The number of realms is inconceivable.
> Just like pictures
> Drawn by an artist
> So are all worlds
> Made by the painter-mind....
> The borders of all the worlds
> Are draped with lotus nets;
> Their various features different
> Their adornments are all pure.[74]

Cook's observation makes the point succinctly:

> The Huayan universe as described by philosophers was meant to be a description of existence as seen in the light of *prajñā*, i.e., as a Buddha sees it.... Philosophy grows out of the experience and then leads back to experience, a finger pointing to the moon of interior space.[75]

The historical evidence bears out the connection between Huayan and the inner world of Zen awakening. Chinul's comment is representative here:

> I had always had doubts about the approach to entering into awakening in the Huayan teachings: what, finally, did it involve? Accordingly, I decided to question a [Huayan] lecturer. He replied, "You must contemplate the unimpeded interpenetration of all phenomena." He entreated me further: "If you merely contemplate your own mind and do not contemplate the unimpeded interfusion of all phenomena, you will never gain the perfect qualities of the fruition of Buddhahood."
>
> I did not answer, but thought silently to myself, "If you use the mind to contemplate phenomena, those phenomena will become impediments and you will have needlessly disturbed your own mind; when will there ever be an end to this situation? But if the mind is brightened and your wisdom purified, then one hair and all the universe will be interfused for there is, perforce, nothing which is outside [the mind]." I then retired into the mountains and sat reading through the *Tripitaka* in search of a passage which would confirm the mind-doctrine [of Zen].[76]

An essential aspect of Huayan thought is that all beings in the three worlds—the world of desire, the world of form, and the world of the formless—are only in the mind.[77] The assertion that all things in the phenomenal world arise together in an unobstructed mutual relationship—"the dependent origination of *dharmadātu*"[78]—can also be said of "the essence and function of one's own mind."[79]

We only exists in relationship with others, and through them to the whole. Not even our relationship to ourselves is exempt from this condition. The idea of emptiness and the idea of dependent origination are two sides of the same coin. In this sense, we may say that Huayan thought includes the three equiprimordial dimensions of our experience of ultimate reality: the existential, the social, and the religious.[80] Each jewel in Indra's net is related inwardly to itself, stands in limitless social relations with others, and reflects the whole in itself. When these three dimensions are seen integrated as equally fundamental, we arrive at the realization that wisdom and compassion are one and the same.

Insofar as the Christian faith enjoins believers to decenter themselves before God and Christ, it confirms the Buddhist way of being and thinking expressed in the philosophy of *śūnyatā*.[81] Consequently, if it is true that there is no fixed center in the world that holds everything in existence, the inverse would also be true: everything that exists is the center through which everything else can be said to exist.

Philosophical insight into the nonsubstantiality or no-self of all things reaches its peak in the Huayan Buddhist vision of reality as a boundless sphere of interactional identity and total intercausality" in which there is no absolute center—or, if there is one, a center that is everywhere.[82] Simply put, the image of Indra's net exposes the idea of a sole causal agent as a fiction.

The Buddhist insight that all causality in the world is governed by the law of karma suggests a comparison with Greek tragedy's influence on the emergence of natural science in the West. Buddhism's "mechanical worldview" leaves no room for a personal God to explain the origin of the world and the way to relieve suffering.

The Buddhist ideas of *śūnyatā* and no-self, as we have seen, are a radical form of decentering the human. The problem is how to integrate this standpoint with the decentering of the human brought about by the advance of modern natural science. The Buddhist worldview reaffirms the need for religion and science to collaborate like "two half-circles" in "circuminsessional interpenetration" in a new appreciation of human beings and their place within the natural world.

ENTERING THE DHĀTU OF FAITHS:
TOWARDS "A THEOLOGY OF PLURALISTIC PLURALISM"

We cannot afford to allow the theological understanding of religion to be defined by the question of whether or not there is only one ultimate religious truth.[83] For Asian Christians, the problem is both a distraction and an abstraction. There is no way to answer it definitively, and in any case, it has no ultimate meaning for their faith. In theory, pluralism can be defined as "the metaphysical doctrine that all existence is ultimately reducible to a multiplicity of distinct and independent beings or elements.[84] In practice, however, we know that Asian Christians assimilate a multiplicity of faiths into their own faith. The question of whether or not there is a single, supreme truth that transcends all epistemological variations is a question that cannot be asked and answered without objectifying the plurality of religious traditions and bracketing the reality of how the faith is practiced. No matter how we choose to formulate the dichotomy between the One and the many, it is no longer a valid model for understanding the lived reality of religious pluralism. The fact is, one faith consists of many religions, and many religions are expressed in one faith.

To be honest to the pluralist reality of Christianity, theology needs to take the following steps. First, theology must distance itself from any exclusive, dogmatic approach to other religious traditions. Troeltsch's "historical method," Hick's "pluralistic hypothesis," and Knitter's "unitive pluralism" have all made important strides toward displacing a self-centered view of religion with a reality-centered one. Hick's focus on a transcendent One above and beyond all historical and cultural-religious phenomena, for example, offers a provisional means (what Buddhism refers to as *upāya*) to that end.

Second, theology should cut the thread that is thought to tie all the religious traditions of the world to the same transcendent One. Nishitani's standpoint of the emptiness of all things leads us to detach ourselves from the oneness of reality by accepting the emptiness of emptiness itself and refusing to transform *śūnyatā* into a unifying principle or supreme One beyond all beings. It is neither a simple negation of beings nor a transcendent substance, but only a name for the dependent origination of everything that makes up reality. It is neither dualistic nor monistic. In other words, the standpoint of *śūnyatā* is the standpoint of *Dharma*, the universal truth that surpasses individuals without dissolving them into an all-encompassing, eternal nothingness. The Dharma becomes Dharma only in the self, "in one's own subjectivity." Indeed, *Śūnyatā* is manifest in all phenomena just as they are—and only there. In no sense is it a unifying principle that grounds the totality of all beings. The Buddhist philosopher Abe Masao comments:

> Oneness as a universal principle, if substantial and self-existing, must be overcome; otherwise we as particulars lose our individuality and cannot possibly awaken to Reality. From the Buddhist point of view, this is true even for God, the "only One." On the other hand, if all particular things are respectively self-identical, there is no equality between them and everything is self-centered. Both Emptiness, the negation of oneness, and egolessness, the negation of everything's self-centeredness, are necessary for Awakening.[85]

The discussion over "multiple religious belonging" brings the abstract question of religious pluralism closer to lived experience. To those accustomed to a monocentric identity, having a single axis around which all one's thoughts and beliefs rotate—be it faith or reason or the mystique of the divine—gives a sense of comfort and security by coercing reality into an idea of oneness tailored to dispel doubt with certitude. Nishitani explains:

> This also explains why it is that the absolute One is inevitably conceived of as something abstracted from the multiplicity and differentiations of all beings. In a system of being that excludes nothingness, the idea that "all beings are One" leads to the positing of a One seen as mere non-differentiation. It is precisely from this sort of standpoint that absolute unity is symbolized as a circle or sphere.[86]

In contrast, the standpoint of emptiness is a "field of dispersion," because it cracks the One open to disclose up to the nihility at the bottom of one's existence. To illustrate his point, Nishitani invites us not to see a circle "from within the circle itself, but as something that includes tangents at all points on the circumference." By doing that, we come to realize "that all those points imply an absolute negation of the orientation to revert to oneness at the center (the orientation given to them as properties of a circle), such that each point implies an orientation toward infinite dispersion."[87] If we look at the center of the circle from a position on the circumference, our sight converges on that single center. It reduces the many to one and overlooks the multiplicity and differentiation of points on the circumference. But if, from that same position, we concentrate attention on the multitude of points on the circumference, we see through the idea of a single center as a mere figment of the imagination. Instead, we see every point on the circumference scattering endlessly in all directions. To see the many from the many is to deconstruct the standpoint of the oneness into an infinite differentiation and multiplicity. By embracing a "great doubt" about the oneness of reality, the nihility at the ground and center of being is laid open before one:

> Furthermore, when the unique existence of all things and multiplicity and differentiation in the world appear on the field of nihility, all things appear isolated from one another by an abyss. Each thing has its being as a one-and-only, a solitariness absolutely shut up within itself. We call such a state of absolute self-enclosure "nihilistic." In human awareness, this solitariness is expressed as being suspended, all alone, over a limitless void.... On the field of nihility, though, all nexus and unity is broken down and the self-enclosure of things is absolute. All things that are scatter apart from one another endlessly. And even the "being" of each thing that is shatters in every direction, riding atop its tangents, as it were, of which we know not whence they come nor whither they go. This existence seems to evaporate into a bottomless nihility; its possibility of existence seems to continually sink away into an impossibility of existence.[88]

To step away from the standpoint of oneness that diminishes the centrality of every concrete point of existence, we need first to accept each being as an absolute center, and then to step onto the field of the nihility where that very centrality is absolutely negated.

Accordingly, we have to eliminate any idea of an a priori transcendent One in the field of nihility as a means to unify all the various religious traditions. Only then can we be said to enter into the *dhātu* of faiths on the Huayan Buddhist model. In this realm, an *outer* religious pluralism is embodied somatically into an *inner* religious pluralism that corresponds to the way it is actually experienced in persons of faith, namely, the way Monica Coleman speaks of individuals or entire communities who "live and function as members of multiple religious traditions simultaneously."[89]

Here again, it is important to recall that the standpoint of emptiness rejects the idea of a mere "dispersion," where every scattered point becomes an ultimate center within a circumferenceless circle. Not to do so would make nihility into a self-enclosed absolute. Nishitani explains:.

> The field of *śūnyatā* is a void of infinite space, without limit or orientation, a void in which the circles and all the tangents that intersect them come into being. Here the mode of being of things as they are in themselves, even though it arise from the sort of center where "All are One," is not reduced to a One that has had all multiplicity and differentiation extracted from it. Since there is no circumference on the field of *śūnyatā*, "All are One" cannot be symbolized by a circle (or sphere).[90]

How might we then imagine a world where the self-closed circle is broken into an endless number of points at the circumference? Because there is no longer any circumference, the circle cannot be defined, and without a definition, there is nowhere to position the multitude of points or indeed any center. If we can speak of a *center* at all, it must be a center that is everywhere. "Each and every thing becomes the center of all things and, in that sense, becomes an absolute center. This is the absolute uniqueness of things, their reality." Nishitani paraphrases this in Huayan terms:

> We may call this relationship, which is only possible on the field of *śūnyatā* "circuminsessional." To say that a certain thing is situated in a position of servant to every other thing means that it lies at the ground of all other things, that it is a constitutive element in the being of every other thing, making it to be what it is and thus to be situated in a position of autonomy as master of itself. It assumes a position at the home-ground of every other thing as that of a retainer upholding his lord.[91]

To identify this field of emptiness a *dhātu* of faiths is to see each faith as in some sense "hybrid." In other words, multiple religious identities can be said to constitute a single faith in a "circuminsessional" way.

What is the best theological paradigm to expresses the religious nature of pluralism? I suggest we call it a "theology of pluralistic pluralism" to signal another *salto mortale* beyond Knitter's "theology of unitive pluralism," which stands in the tradition of Troeltsch's model of the One and the many. In his autobiographical work *Without Buddha I could not be a Christian*, Knitter presents the position of "double-religious belonging" as a practical consequence of his idea of unitive pluralism. The joint fidelity to Christian and

Buddhist traditions that he advances after years of reflection and debate is accomplished more naturally by Asian believers for whom the claim "I could not be Christian without the religious influence of my culture" is a matter of everyday wisdom.

The theology of pluralistic pluralism as I understand it here also manifests the kind of "non-dualistic pluralism" we saw in Panikkar's advaitic standpoint. This is to clarify from the outset that there is no intention of promoting unity among different religions or arguing metaphysically for the plurality of truth. I mean to insist only that each religion provides a "center" around which believers can integrate their self-understanding. Such a center does not, however, preclude the possibility of other centers. In this sense, we might say that a pluralistic pluralism assumes that a center is both a center and, at the same time, a circumference for other centers. Or better, a center is first truly a center not when it defines itself in opposition to other centers but only when it serves as a circumference for them. From such a perspective, each religion is, as it were, one heliocentric universe among many. Panikkar explains:

> As long as we entertain a mechanocentric conception and a geometrical notion of reality, a number of problems are exceedingly complicated and can hardly find any solution. Either Christians "stick" to their "Christ" and become exclusive, or they give up their claims, dilute their beliefs, and become, at best, inclusivistic. These two horns of dilemma are equally unacceptable. The parallel Copernican revolution consists in shifting the center from linear history to an anthrocosmic vision, a kind of trinitarian notion, not of the godhead alone, but of reality. The center is neither the earth (our particular religion), nor the sun (God, transcendence, the Absolute). Rather, each solar system has its own center, and every galaxy turns reciprocally around the other. There is no absolute center. Reality itself is concentric inasmuch as each being (each tradition) is the center of the universe—of its own universe to begin with. The anthrocosmic insight (which sees the unity between the divine-human cosmos) suggests a sort of trinitarian dynamism in which all is implied in all (each person represents the community and each tradition reflects, corrects, complements, and challenges the other).[92]

A true *dhātu* of faiths cannot be understood on the model of a unitive pluralism in which the rich variety of religious understanding combines to form a single whole. Neither can it be reduced to a theocentric or reality-centered plurality along the lines of Hick's model. The only way to grasp a world of multiple faiths in its lived reality is to accept it as an advaitic plurality or pluralistic pluralism—that is, to transcend the dichotomy between a unity that denies plurality and a plurality that denies all forms of unity. The former leads to imperialistic modes of thought; the latter, to the dismissal of interreligious dialogue and cooperation as mere illusion.

A theology of pluralistic pluralism approaches our experience of the unimpeded and mutual penetration of the religious traditions in the outer world of history and culture as well as in inner world of personal faith. As we have shown in the case of Nishitani, the nihilism born of modern science lead one to a field of emptiness, where the indifference of God's love and the indifference of the laws of nature can be affirmed simultaneously by those awakened to the groundlessness of existence. The commitment to a pluralistic pluralism goes hand in hand with the scientific demand for a continued demythologizing of superhistorical and supernatural religious objects. Moreover, encountering other religious traditions and natural science as genuinely theological challenges helps us break free of an unhealthy attachment to an overbearing, authoritative One as the only authentic form of unity. Unlike a unitive pluralism, a pluralistic pluralism allows the many to be many. It allows faith to be experienced for what it is and always must be, consciously or unconsciously: a faith among faiths.

⋮

Any conclusion to be drawn from these pages is at best provisional and expressed as another question. We have, after all, been caught up in a chain of questions not of our own making but received from the past. To live in history and bring that history to life in ourselves is to reinforce our questions about the things that matter most by foregoing answers that draw them to a conclusion.

In Case 45 of the twelfth-century collection of Zen kōan known as the *Blue Cliff Record*, the following exchange takes place between a monk and his master:

> A monk asked Zhaozhou,
> "All dharmas are reduced to oneness,
> but what is oneness reduced to?"

> Zhaozhou said,
> "When I was in Qingzhou
> I made a hempen shirt.
> It weighed seven pounds."[93]

Typical of such exchanges, there appears to be no logical connection between the monk's question and the master's reply. Zhaozhou does not say what oneness is reduced to or where. It subverts the assumption on which the question is based, that all things (dharmas) can be reduced to one.

It is not hard to imagine the consternation of the monk at not having his problem taken seriously. He is left adrift without an answer and without a question. This sense of total deprivation and disorientation is an image of what a heightened awareness of history and nature has done to human self-understanding in the modern age. The quest of ultimate oneness that once defined us seems to have crumbled to dust in our hands.

Our examination of Nishitani's "standpoint of emptiness" and the Huayan Buddhist understanding of *dharamadhātu* suggests that the nihility we experience for having lost our way is not a permanent state of confinement but an opportunity to turn the nihilism that has overtaken us against itself by affirming it and at the same time denying its ultimate hold over us. This is the place from which the theology of pluralistic pluralism stands in affirming the reality of many faiths while denying the loss of the traditional claim to absolute truth and the power of pluralism to intimidate or enfeeble our own faith. Far from being left adrift and disoriented with questions for which we have no answer, the awareness of Christianity as a faith among faiths changes the question to echo the words of Karl Löwith:

> How could the Christian pilgrimage *in hoc saeculo* ever become homeless in a land where it has never been at home?[94]

Notes

1. Religion and Science as *loci theologici*

1. GADAMER 2004, 83. See. OTT, 17.
2. See HEIDEGGER 1962, 182. Cf. OTT 1967, 194; 1968, 101.
3. GADAMER 2004, 250.
4. GADAMER 2004, 261. Gadamer is commenting here on Heidegger's analysis of *Dasein*.
5. All biblical quotations in this book follow the New Revised Standard Edition.
6. OTT 1967, 190 (emphasis added).
7. GADAMER 2004, 301.
8. GADAMER 2004, 300.
9. OTT 1968, 101.
10. CELAN 1983, 185–6.
11. GADAMER 1973, 12.
12. GADAMER 2004, 378.
13. LOHSE 1983, 23–4.
14. LOHSE 1983, 24 (emphasis added).
15. ARISTOTLE 1960, 273.
16. GADAMER 1992, 346.
17. CICERO 2003, 117.
18. CICERO 2003, 7.
19. ARISTOTLE, *Topica* viii,14 163b (1960, 20–30). See also CARRUTHERS 1990, 104ff.
20. LEFF 1983, 23.
21. CICERO, *De oratore*, II.174 (1967, 323).
22. Regarding the broad influence of CURTIUS's work on European academia, see RICH-ARDS 1983. The reception was not unlike that accorded Thomas Kuhn's *The Structure of Scientific Revolution* after its publication in 1962—except for theology which kept silent rather than weigh in on the controversy over "topics." As Karl LEHMANN remarks, this is odd, given that "from its first beginnings Christian theology has long been familiar with topical thinking" (LEHMANN 1988, 520).
23. CURTIUS 2013, 79.
24. CURTIUS 2013, 82.
25. CURTIUS 2013, 23.
26. CURTIUS 2013, 18.
27. CURTIUS 1938, 139.
28. CURTIUS 2013, 79.

29. FRANK 2017, 204ff.

30. VICO 1948, 82.

31. GADAMER 2004, 20.

32. GADAMER 2004, 22.

33. HEIDEGGER 1962, 178.

34. HEIDEGGER 2002, 110.

35. GADAMER, 1977, 96.

36. SCHOLZ 2015, 489; FRANK 2012, 1–10.

37. PREUS 2014, 2.

38. GADAMER 1976, 283.

39. KLINGER, 1978, 13.

40. BRETZKE 1998, 79. See also LEHMANN 1988.

41. WERBICK 2015, 64.

42. BARBOUR 1990, xiii.

43. BARBOUR 1990, xv.

44. PETERS 2018, 42–3.

45. PETERS 2018, 33.

46. DREES 2010, 106–8.

47. BARBOUR 1966, 453–4.

48. I am paraphrasing S. N. BALAGANGAHARA (2012, 5) who comments on the Western construction of the image of India that "what the Europeans think they know of India tells us more about Europe than it does about India." The same kind of self-deception is at work in the theological expropriation of the dialogue between religion and science.

49. HEIDEGGER 1962, 536.

50. VON WEIZSÄCKER 1949, 5–6.

51. VON WEIZSÄCKER 1991, 98.

52. See GADAMER 2004, 305.

53. GADAMER 2004, 264.

54. VON WEIZSÄCKER 1991, 288–9.

55. VON WEIZSÄCKER 1991, 98.

56. VON WEIZSÄCKER 1991, 217.

57. DAMPIER 1929.

58. See LOVEJOY 1960.

59. HARRISON 2000, 19.

60. VON WEIZSÄCKER 1991, 29.

61. JONAS 1994, 85–7.

62. DENNETT 1995, 21.

63. MONOD 1971, xi.

64. DARWIN 2009, 423.

65. DARWIN 2009, 39.

66. RUSSELL 1935, 76.

67. MAYR 1991, ix.

68. HICK 2006, xi.

69. SAITŌ and SASAKI 2009, 45–9.

70. HICK 2006, 42. The tack Hick follows in his defense of the theology against brain science's attack reminds us of position taken by theological discourse against logical positivism. See HICK 1990, 100–3.

71. HICK 2006, 205.

72. HICK 2006, 206.

73. INGRAM 2008, 15.

74. INGRAM 2008, 110.

75. INGRAM 2008, 132. Amos Yong's work, *The Cosmic Breath* defines its task in terms sympathetic to our task here: "What does it mean to do theology in a pluralistic world of modern science?" (YONG 2012, 1). Unfortunately, the results do not measure up to the author's ambitions. Theologically, his Christian-Buddhist-science "trialogue" stands on different ground from that of Hick and Ingram, given his prior avowal of a "Spirit hermeneutics" and its unabashed commitment to "understand the human ultimate concern within a theistic framework" (see YONG 2003, 17). He sees his idea through with the help of Phillip Clayton's "emergence theory," which argues for the sudden and discontinuous emergence of more complicated structures of reality. Convinced that emergence theory offers a solid scientific explanation for the creative action of the Spirit in the material world, he takes it up as a pivotal meeting point for Christian faith and natural science. However, as Drees has pointed out, it is hard to dispossess emergence theory of its materialism, given that it seeks to describe "how complex behavior arises in and through material structures" (DREES 2009, 33–4). In a word, Yong's theological endeavors seem to land him far from his intended goal, in an arbitray transference of scientific words and ideas into theology. See LEIDENHAG 2015.

2. Placing Christianity in History

1. KNITTER 1985, 23.

2. PANNENBERG 1979, 253.

3. PANNENBERG 1979, 253 (emphasis added). Pannenberg's critique of the theology of Word of God is aimed at Rudolf Bultman's understanding of the history. Relying on Hegel's concept of "universal history," Pannenberg insists that the Christian faith should not be based on the existential history of the faith, as it is in Bultmann's case, but on a "universal" that includes both the history of faith and secular history. In this sense, Pannenberg's theological project of interpreting "revelation as history" falls in the tradition of German idealism. See PANNENBERG 1961.

4. TILLICH 1967, 245.

5. TILLICH 1964, 43. Cf. THOMAS 1995, 24–5.

6. TILLICH, 1924, 351.

7. TROELTSCH 1925, 3.

8. TROELTSCH 1922, 9.

9. TROELTSCH 1913, 730.

10. TROELTSCH 1913, 5.

11. TROELTSCH 1913, 6.

12. TROELTSCH 1913, 1. Cf. TROELTSCH 1971, 47–8.

13. TROELTSCH 1980, 11.

14. "Thinkers no longer took the cosmos as their starting point in order to demonstrate in a quasi-experimental way that God is the first cause of the natural order. Instead, they argued from the existence and experience of human beings in order to show that God is inevitably presupposed in every act of human existence.... The growing anthropocentrism that has marked the development of Christian theology has not, however, been due solely to the influence of philosophy. It has also had another and genuinely theological cause: the fact that Christian theology is a response to the human question of salvation" (

15. TROELTSCH 1913, 5.

16. TROELTSCH 1925, 9.

17. TROELTSCH 1971, 47–8.

18. TROELTSCH 1971, 97.

19. TROELTSCH 1971, 110–11.

20. TROELTSCH 1971, 114.

21. TROELTSCH 1971, 111–13. Interestingly enough, we can find the same rhetoric of personalistic-ethical Christianity levelled against the impersonalistic-logical religions in a lecture by Albert Schweitzer on Christianity and religions of the world. Cf. SCHWEITZER 1974.

22. VON HÜGEL 1924, vii.

23. TROELTSCH 1980, 22.

24. TROELTSCH 1980, 29.

25. TROELTSCH 1980, 29–30.

26. TROELTSCH 1980, 31 (emphasis added)

27. RACE 1983.

28. KNITTER 1985, 27.

29. IGGERS 1983, 195

30. ODAGAKI 1983, 206.

31. Cf. SMITH 1998; MASUZAWA 2005, 309ff.

32. HEILER 1961, 17.

33. TROELTSCH 1925, 4 (emphasis added).

34. MASUZAWA 2005, 312–3.

35. KUHN 1962, 148.

36. COLEMAN 2011, 6–7 (emphasis added).

37. COLEMAN 2011, 9.

38. KNITTER 2009, 214. On the issue of "multiple religions belonging," see CORNILLE 2003; BERNHARDT and SCHMIDT-LEUKEL 2008; PHAN 2003.

39. HUSTWIT 2017, 108.

40. WUTHNOW 1998, 2; see also BERGER 2005.

41. VAN BRAGT 2003. See also HEDGES 2017, ASMARA 2017.

42. VAN BRAGT 2014, 37.

43. VAN BRAGT 2014, 39.

44. Endō's last novel, *Deep River*, which shows considerable influence from the religious pluralism of John Hick

45. ENDŌ 1969, 293.

46. HONDA 1973, 2; cited in VAN BRAGT 2014, 39.

47. VAN BRAGT 2014, 40.

48. KEEL 1996, 185.

49. KIM 1996, 92–3.

50. Sun Hwan Pyun was a theologian of the Korean Methodist Church and a leading voice for indigenous theology. His views on Religious pluralism led to his excommunication and a sudden death prevented him from developing his theological thought further.

51. PYUN 1996, 180–1 (emphasis added).

52. The passage is from Freud's *Introductory Lectures on Psychoanalysis* and is cited here from GOULD 1987. Gould includes a third "outrage," the geological discoveries of fossils that brought human beings face to face with "deep time":

> What could be more comforting, what more convenient for human domination, than the traditional concept of young earth, ruled by the Human will within days of its origin. How threatening, by contrast, the notion of an almost incomprehensible immensity, with human habitation restricted to a millimicrosecond at the very end! (GOULD 1987, 2)

53. BALDI 2001, 10–12.

54. See KIM 2009.

55. BALDI 2001, 5.

56. BALDI 2001, 68.

57. BALDI 2001, 66.

58. BALDI 2001, 3–4.

59. VON WEIZSÄCKER 1991, 213.

60. RAHNER 1983, 16.

61. PANNENBERG 1985, 27.

62. SCHELER 1976, 120

63. SCHELER 2009, 5–6

64. SCHELER 2009, 5.

65. SCHELER 2009, 6.

66. SCHELER 2009, 6–7.

67. SCHELER 2009, 7.

68. SCHELER 2009, 16 (emphasis added).

69. SCHELER 2009, 26.

70. SCHELER 2009, 50.

71. SCHELER 2009, 27.

72. SCHELER 2009, 42.

73. SCHELER 2009, 43–4.

74. SCHELER 2009, 44.

75. GEHLEN 1988, 13.

76. WILSON 1998, 8.

77. WILSON 1978, 172.

78. WILSON 1978, 127. Cf. RUSE and WILSON 1986, 180.

79. DENNETT, 2006, 4.

80. DENNETT, 2006 25.

81. DENNETT, 2006, 17.

82. LAWSON 2000, 344.
83. GUTHRIE 1980, 187.
84. BARRETT 2000, 31.
85. BOYER 2003, 123.
86. SHULTS 2014, 3.
87. BOYER 2002, 32.
88. BOYER 2002, 33.
89. BOYER 2002, 78.
90. BOYER 2002 133.
91. BOYER 2002, 131.
92. BOYER 2002, 158.
93. BOYER 2002, 129–30.
94. BOYER 2002, 157.

3. Dwelling in the Negative

1. LUEHRS 1975, 16.
2. LÖWITH 1964, 388.
3. OVERBECK 1995, 4: 44.
4. Cf. SOMMER 1997.
5. LÖWITH 1964, 385.
6. LÖWITH 1964, 379.
7. OVERBECK 2005, 40.
8. SCHÜTZ 1963, 417.
9. OVERBECK 1995, 5: 491.
10. LÖWITH 1964, 387.
11. LÖWITH 1964, 387. Cf. NIGG 2009, 165ff.
12. OTT 1988, 184.
13. BARTH 1933, 252.
14. Cf. WOLFE 2013, 31.
15. PÖGGELER 1983, 36, 318.
16. PETER 2000, 107.
17. LUEHRS 1975, 17.
18. HIGASHI 1975, 55ff. Heidegger depicts the possibility of inheritance of a tradition in relation with the existential "anticipatory resoluteness" and the rebirth of an "authentic" existence as follows:

> Anticipatory resoluteness brings this Being-towards-death into authentic existence. The historizing of this resoluteness, however, is the repetition of the heritage of possibilities by handing these down to oneself in anticipation; and we have interpreted this historizing as authentic historicality.... In the fateful repetition of possibilities that have been, Dasein brings itself back "immediately"—that is to say, in a way that is temporally ecstatical—to what already has been before it. But when its heritage is thus handed down to itself, its "birth" is caught up into its existence in coming back from

the possibility of death (the possibility which is not to be outstripped), if only so that this existence may accept the thrownness of its own "there" in a way which is more free from Illusion. (HEIDEGGER 1962, 442–3).

19. "Domestication" (*Zähmung*) is a key concept in Peter Sloterdijk's argument for the similarity between the Western tradition of humanism and the technology of human cloning. Quoting HEIDEGGER's essay, "Brief über den Humanismus," he maintains that humanism, the ongoing attempts to eliminate or domesticate beast in our natures through education, had resulted in total failure. He suggests present-day biotechnology like cloning as a viable alternative in that it would bring our genetically inherited nature under our own control for our own good. His opinion prompted a strong controversy with Jürgen Habermas. Cf. SLOTERDIJK 1999: HABERMAS 2005.

20. PENCE 2002, 57.

21. PETERS 1997, 12.

22. Cf. Kim 2009, in which I explain the response of Christian theologies on a number of biotechnological issues, among which I single out the cloning of living things (including human beings). Broadly speaking there are three approaches to the idea of "playing God" through cloning: "We ought not play God" (Paul Ramsey), "Are we really playing God when we clone humans?"(Ted Peters), and "Let's play God!" (Joseph Fletcher). Each of these positions, of course, has its own style of argument. Paul Ramsey relies on Barth's theology of the Word of God, which underscore underlines the absolute otherness of the transcendent God. Ted Peters owes his flexible approach to cloning to his sympathy for Wolfhart Pannenberg's view of history as eschatological openness. Finally, Joseph Fletcher, the author of *Situation Ethics: The New Morality* (1966) and *The Ethics of Genetic Control: Ending Reproductive Roulette* (1974), was an active advocate of a secular theology that emphasizes the responsibility of human beings in the age of the death of God.

If there is no God and therefore no higher spiritual realm, what are we to make of Dostoevsky's warning that if God does not exist, then everything is permitted? If it is said that human beings, as creatures of God, are not allowed to play God, what happens if God has no role to play either? From what perspective should we make ethical judgments about scientists' work if there is no higher source of moral boundaries? Is it even possible to speak of transgressing boundaries if the boundaries themselves are fluid? All of this leads us back to the need for clarifying what religion is and how it should respond to scientific modes of truth. That the perspectives of science and religion do not coincide is obvious, but that does not exclude the possibility of dialogue.

23. WILMUT, CAMPBELL, and TUDGE 2000, 3.

24. ŽIŽEK 2004, 123.

25. ŽIŽEK 2004, 123.

26. See n. 19 above.

27. ŽIŽEK 2004 123–4.

28. "But the life of mind is not one that shuns death, and keeps clear of destruction; it endures death and in death maintains its being. It only wins to its truth when it finds itself utterly torn asunder. It is this mighty power, not by being a positive which turns away from the negative, as when we say of anything it is nothing or it is false, and, being then done with it, pass off to something else: on the contrary, mind is this power only by looking the negative

in the face, and dwelling with it. This dwelling beside it is the magic power that converts the negative into being. That power is just what we spoke of above as subject, which by giving determinateness a place in its substance, cancels abstract immediacy, i.e. immediacy which merely is, and, by so doing, becomes the true substance, becomes being or immediacy that does not have mediation outside it, but is this mediation itself" (HEGEL 2003, 18–19).

29. CHINUL 1983, 97, 127.

30. CHINUL 1983, 97.

31. CHINUL 1983, 127. Zen master Dōgen (1200–1253), founder of the Japanese Sōtō School, comments on the phrase cited by Chinul:

> There is an ancient saying that came from India and China: "If something falls to the earth it will surely arise."... Therefore, if you are asked, "How can we accomplish the Buddhist Way?" you can answer, "It is like arising from the earth after you have fallen." In order to understand this clearly you must be detached from the illusion of past, present, and future. Enlightenment is to transcend enlightenment; to go thoroughly into illusion is to transcend illusion and to arrive at great enlightenment. You are covered with either enlightenment or illusion; your condition depends on the principle of falling and arising from the earth.... However, if you do not understand this, when you fall to the earth you can never arise. (DŌGEN 1975, "Suchness," sec. 17)

32. NISHITANI 1940, 11–12.

33. Cf. ECKHART 2009, 298.

34. PANIKKAR 1999, 4.

35. PANIKKAR 1999, 4 (emphasis added).

36. PANIKKAR 1995, 172.

37. PANIKKAR 1975, 166.

38. PANIKKAR 1995, 173

39. PANIKKAR 1995, 146.

40. PANIKKAR 1995, 172.

41. FRANK 2011.

42. GGW 2: 384. GRONDIN 2003, 60.

43. PANIKKAR 2010, 338.

44. OTT 1988, 194 (emphasis added).

45. OTT 1959, 72.

46. OTT 1959, 72.

47. HEIDEGGER 1993, 95.

48. OTT 1959, 102ff.

49. NUSSBAUM 1990, 4.

50. NUSSBAUM 1990, 3.

51. MERLEAU-PONTY 1964, 26.

52. MERLEAU-PONTY 1964, 28.

53. NUSSBAUM 1990, 4–5.

54. 水到渠成. See NISHITANI 1982, 28.

55. PACI 1998.

56. For experiments in developing a style of theological writing suited to the encounter with religion and science, see KIM 1998 and 2012.

4. The Topos of Śūnyatā

1. For a brief biography of Nishitani, see HEISIG 2001, 183–7; ŌHASHI 2011, 237ff.

2. 空の立場.

3. Nishitani lived in Germany from 1937 to 1939, during which time he conducted research under Martin Heidegger, who was then lecturing on Nietzsche.

4. HEISIG 2001, 191.

5. HEISIG 2001, 245–9.

6. NISHITANI 1986, 24.

7. I borrow this word from Clifford Geertz, who defines religion as a cultural system:

A religion is a system of symbols which acts to establish powerful, pervasive, and long-lasting moods in men by formulating conceptions of a general order of existence and clothing those conceptions with such an aura of factuality that the moods and motivations seem uniquely realistic. (GEERTZ 1973, 90

8. This term for describing the relationship between religion and science, was adapted by Nishitani's translator, Jan Van Bragt, from its original theological use to explain the relationship among the persons of the Trinity. See NISHITANI 1982, 294–5.

9. VAN BRAGT, 1982, xxxvi.

10. NISHITANI 1982, 47.

11. NIETZSCHE 1974, 181.

12. NISHITANI 1982, 57.

13. NISHITANI 1940, 19.

14. NISHITANI 1982, 90.

15. NISHITANI 1940, 65.

16. NISHITANI 1982, 179.

17. HEISIG 2001, 193.

18. PARKES 1990, xxxi–xxxii.

19. NISHITANI 1990, 82.

20. NISHITANI 2004, 117.

21. BRONOWSKI 1977, 164.

22. NISHITANI 1990, 70–1.

23. NISHITANI 1990, 90.

24. NISHITANI 1990, 50.

25. NISHITANI 1990, 85.

26. NISHITANI 1990, 85–6.

27. HASE 1999, 140.

28. NISHITANI 1982, 174.

29. NISHITANI 1990, xxxiii.

30. NISHITANI 1977.

31. "Before you wipe it clean or polish it, this old mirror it reflects heaven and earth. But when you wipe it, it turns completely black."

32. NISHITANI 1985, 4.

33. 大疑.

34. NISHITANI 1986, 27.

35. 大疑現前. NISHITANI 1986, 28.

36. NISHITANI 1986, 3.

37. NISHITANI 1986, 1.

38. NISHITANI 1990, 6–7.

39. See, for example, YUASA 2004.

40. NISHITANI 1990, 82.

41. NISHITANI 1986, 28–9.

42. NISHITANI 1982, 79.

43. NISHITANI 2004, 107.

44. NISHITANI 1982, 53.

45. NISHITANI 2004, 107–8.

46. Nothingness = 無, absolute nothingness = 絶対無; emptiness/ *śūnyatā* = 空.

47. Nihilism is translated into Japanese as 虚無主義, and atheism as 無神論, in both of which the character for nothingness (無) figures.

48. Self-nature/*svabhāva* = 自性

49. *Mūlamadhyamakakārikā* 24.18; KALUPAHANA 1986, 339.

50. Field of emptiness = 空の場; *dharmadhātu* = 法界.

51. COOK 1977, 3; see also KAMATA 1974, 102

52. NISHITANI 1982, 54.

53. HASE 2009, 76.

54. HASE 1999, 144.

55. HASE 1999, 145 (wording adjusted).

56. NISHITANI 1982, 97.

57. NISHITANI 1982, 98.

58. NISHITANI 1982, 90.

59. NISHITANI 1982, 50.

60. NISHITANI 1982, 53.

61. NISHITANI 1982, 50.

62. NISHITANI 1982, 52.

63. NISHITANI 1982, 93–4.

64. NISHITANI 1982, 97.

65. NISHITANI 1982, 94.

66. NISHITANI 1982, 96–7.

67. NISHITANI 1982, 52.

68. NISHITANI 1982, 49.

69. WHITEHEAD 1925, 11.

70. NISHITANI 1982, 98.

71. NISHITANI 1982, 106.

72. SUZUKI Kō, 1983, 321.

73. NISHITANI 1982, 58.

74. NISHITANI 1982, 97.

75. NISHITANI 1982, 40–1.

76. NISHITANI 1982, 58–9.

77. NISHITANI 1982, 48.

78. VATTIMO 1988, 19. In his essay "An Apology for Nihilism," Vattimo agrees with Nietzsche that being an "accomplished nihilist" is the one chance left for us. According to a note at the beginning of *Wille zur Macht*, nihilism describes "the situation in which man rolls from the center toward x." In this regard, Nietzsche and Heidegger are seen to coincide: for the former, x is the death of God and the devaluation of the highest values; for the latter, it is the reduction of Being to value (20).

In his analysis of *Being and Time*, Nishitani writes:

> Heidegger gives us nothing less than an ontology within which nihilism becomes a philosophy. By disclosing nothing at the ground of all beings and summoning it forth, nihilism becomes the basis of a new metaphysics. (NISHITANI 1990, 157)

This agrees with Vattimo's reading of the "nihilistic" aspects of Heidegger's hermeneutics that begin with "his analysis of Dasein as a hermeneutic totality," but lead to the conclusion that "Dasein may be a totality only by anticipating, and resolving upon, its death" (VATTIMO 1988, 115)

79. NISHITANI 1982, 98.

80. See pages 139ff below.

81. NISHITANI 1982, 148.

1. HEISIG 2012, 97.

5. A *Dhātu* of Faiths

2. RACE 1983, x-xi (emphasis added).

3. WHITEHEAD 1925, 49–50.

4. KNITTER 1985, 23.

5. TROELTSCH 1980, 31 (emphasis added).

6. HAYNES 2009, 6.

7. Cf. KÜNG 1993.

8. ASSMANN 2005, 19.

9. ASSMANN 1992, 19–21.

10. SCHMIT 1932, 14.

11. ALTHAUS 2007, 481.

12. HUNTINGTON 2004, 24.

13. ASSMANN 2005, 25.

14. ASSMANN 2005, 25.

15. ASSMANN 1997, 1–2

16. ASSMANN 1997, 210.

17. ASSMANN 1997, 4.

18. ASSMANN 2010, 23.

19. ASSMANN 2010, 16.

20. BECK 2010, 62.

21. BERGER 2005, 6ff.

22. TAYLOR 1984, 14.

23. TAYLOR 1984, 29.

24. TAYLOR 1984, 29.

25. TROELTSCH 1980, 29–30.

26. HICK 1989, 240.

27. KNITTER 1985, 7.

28. KNITTER 1985, 9

29. KNITTER 1985.

30. HICK 1989, 14.

31. HEIM, 1995, 212.

32. HICK 1995, 32.

33. HICK 1995, 40.

34. TAYLOR 1984, 130.

35. TAYLOR 1984, 41–2.

36. COUSINS 1992, 73.

37. PANIKKAR 1999, 2.

38. PANIKKAR 1999, 2.

39. PANIKKAR 1993, 89.

40. CARGAS 1995, vii.

41. PANIKKAR 1979, 381.

42. KNITTER 1996, 178.

43. PANIKKAR 1993, 91.

44. PANIKKAR 1995, 57.

45. PANIKKAR 1993, 109–10, 111.

46. PANIKKAR 1993, 102–7.

47. PANIKKAR 1993, 109. Cf. PANIKKAR 1984, 107ff.

48. PANIKKAR 1993, 110–14.

49. KASULIS 2002, 79.

50. PANIKKAR 1993, 169.

51. See PANIKKAR 1987, 109–10.

52. KIMURA 2004, 525.

53. TAKAKUSU 1973, 29.

54. 諸法実相.

55. 即心是仏.

56. YOSIHARA 1973) 5ff.

57. 華蔵世界.

58. ODIN 1982, 3

59. DUMOULIN 1985, 95.

60. Cited in DUMOULIN 2005, 46–7.

61. KIMURA 2004, 526.

62. 常住論, 断滅論. We do well to recall here that efforts to classify the sutras and their teachings (教相判釈) were undertaken frequently in Buddhism, typically to argue for the superiority of one's own school or a specific sutra. The Huayan school was no exception. However, insofar as the notion of religious pluralism is a modern one, it is pointless, even anachronistic, to apply present-day classifications to ancient traditions. Cf. HAYES 1991, 94–5.

63. COOK 1977, 3.

64. COOK 1977, 4. Cf. KAMATA 1974, 102

65. COOK 1977, 12.

66. TAKEDA 2008, 297

67. COOK 1977, 15.

68. COOK 1977, 48.

69. COOK 1977, 60.

70. COOK 1977, 64–5.

71. COOK 1977, 118.

72. KASULIS 2002, 63.

73. COOK 1977, 30.

74. CLEARY 1984, 244.

75. COOK 1977, 33.

76. *Excerpts from the Exposition of the Avataṃsaka Sūtra*, cited in CHINUL 1983, 24.

77. 三界唯心.

78. 法界縁起. See KAMATA 1974, 95ff.

79. CHINUL 1983, 113.

80. Regarding the term *equiprimordial*, see page 26 above.

81. VON BRÜCK and LAI 1997, 436ff.

82. Cf. NISHIDA 2002, 204.

83. SCHMIDT-LEUKEL 2005, 177.

84. WOODBRIDGE 1981, 66.

85. ABE 1985, 208.

86. NISHITANI 1982, 144.

87. NISHITANI 1982, 143.

88. NISHITANI 1982, 145.

89. See above, page 53.

90. NISHITANI 1982, 146.

91. NISHITANI 1982, 148 (emphasis added).

92. PANIKKAR 1993, 169.

93. SEKIDA 1977, 271. (case 45): 僧問趙州, 萬法歸一, 一歸何處。州云, 我在青州, 作一領佈衫, 重七斤。

94. LÖWITH 1964, 388.

Bibliography

Abbreviations

GGW   Hans-Georg Gadamer, *Gesammelte Werke* (Tübingen: Mohr Siebeck, 1985–2010), 10 vols.

NKC   『西谷啓二著作集』[*Collected Writings of Nishitani Keiji*] (Tokyo: Sōbunsha, 1986–1995), 26 vols.

Other works

ABE Masao 阿部正雄

1985   *Zen and Western Thought* (Hong Kong: Macmillan).

ALTHAUS, Horst

2007   *"Heiden," "Juden," "Christen": Positionen und Kontroversen von Hobbes bis Carl Schmitt* (Würzburg: Königshausen & Neumann).

ARISTOTLE

1960   *Topica*, trans. by E. S. Forster (Cambridge: Harvard University Press).

ASMARA, Alexander Hendra Dwi

2017   "Multiple Religious Belonging and the New Way of Doing Theology," *Jurnal Teologi* 3/2: 153–64.

ASSMANN, Jan

1977   *Moses the Egyptian: The Memory of Egypt in Western Monotheism* (Cambridge, MA: Harvard University Press).

1992   *Das kulturelle Gedächtnins. Schrift, Erinnerung und politische Identität in frühen Hochkulturen* (München: C. H. Beck).

2005   "Monotheismus und die Sprache der Gewalt," in Peter Walter, ed., *Das Gewaltpotential des Monotheismus und der dreieinige Gott* (Freiburg: Herder), 18–38.

2010   *The Price of Monotheism*, trans. by Robert Savage (Stanford: Stanford University Press).

BACKHAUS, Knut

2014   *Religion als Reise: Intertexuelle Lektüren in Antike und Christentum* (Tübingen: Mohr Siebeck).

BALAGANGAHARA, S. N.

2012   *Reconceptualizing India Studies* (Oxford: Oxford University Press).

BALDI, Pierre

    2001   *The Shattered Self: The End of Natural Evolution* (Cambridge, MA: MIT Press).

BARBOUR, Ian

    1966   *Issues in Science and Religion* (New York: Prentice-Hall).

    1990   *Religion and Science: Historical and Contemporary Issues* (San Fransisco: HarperSanFrancisco).

BARRETT, Justin L.

    2000   "Exploring the Natural Foundations of Religion," *Trends in Cognitive Sciences* 4/1: 29–34.

BARTH, Karl

    1933   *The Epistle to the Romans*, trans. E. C. Hoskyns (Oxford: Oxford University Press).

BECK, Ulrich

    2010   *A God of One's Own: Religion's Capacity for Peace and Potential for Violence*, trans. by Rodney Livingstone (Cambridge: Polity).

BERGER, Peter L.

    2005   "Global Pluralism and Religion," *Estudios Públicos* 98: , 1–13.

BERNHARDT, Reinhold and Perry Schmidt-Leukel, eds.

    2008   *Multiple religiöse Identität: Aus verschiedenen religiösen Traditionen schöpfen* (Zürich: Theologischer Verlag Zürich).

BOYER, Pascal

    2002   *Religion Explained: The Evolutionary Origins of Religious Thought* (New York: Basic Books).

    2003   "Religious Thought and Behaviour as By-Products of Brain Function," *Trends in Cognitive Science* 7/3: 119–24.

BRETZKE, James T.

    1998   *Consecrated Phrases: A Latin Theological Dictionary* (Collegeville, MN: Liturgical Press).

BRONOWSKI, Jacob

    1977   *A Sense of the Future: Essays in Natural Philosophy* (Cambridge, MA: MIT Press).

CARGAS, Harry James

    1995   "Introduction," in PANIKKAR 1995, vii–xiv.

CARRUTHERS, Mary J.

    1990   *The Book of Memory: A Study of Memory in Medieval Culture* (Cambridge: Cambridge University Press).

CELAN, Paul

1983 "Ansprache anläßlich der Entgegennahme des Literaturpreises der Freien Hansestadt Bremen (1958)," *Gesammelte Werke, Bd. 3: Gedichte III, Prosa, Reden* (Berlin: Suhrkamp), 185–6.

CHINUL Bojo 普照知訥

1983 「勸修定慧結社文」[Encouragement to practice: The compact of the *samādhi* and *prajñā* community], in Robert E. Buswell, Jr., *The Korean Approach to Zen: The Collected Works of Chinul* (Honolulu: University of Hawaii Press).

CICERO, Marcus Tullius

1967 *De Oratore*, in *Cicero in Twenty-Eight Volumes*, vol. 3, *De Oratore,* Books I and II, trans. by E. W. Sutton (Harvard University Press).

2003 *Topica*, ed. and trans. by Tobias Reinhardt (Oxford University Press).

CLEARY, Thomas, trans.

1984 *The Flower Ornament Scripture: A Translation of the Avatamsaka Sutra* (Shambhala).

COLEMAN, Monica A.

2011 "The Womb Circle: A Womanist Practice of Multi-Religious Belonging," *Practical Matters* 4: 1–9.

COOK, Francis

1977 *Hua-yen Buddhism: The Jewel Net of Indra* (University Park: Pennsylvania State University Press).

CORNILLE, Catherine

2003 (ed.). *Many Mansions? Multiple Religious Belonging and Christian Identity* (New York: Orbis).

COUSINS, Ewert H.

1992 *Christ of the 21st Century* (Rockport, MA: Element).

CURTIUS, Ernst Robert

1938 "Begriff einer historischen Topik" *Zeitschrift für romanische Philologie* 58: 129–42.

1973 *Essays on European Literature*, trans. by Michael Kowel (Princeton: Princeton University Press).

2013 *European Literature and The Latin Middle Ages,* trans. by Willard R. Trask (Princeton: Princeton University Press).

DAMPIER, William C.

1929 *A History of Science and its Relations with Philosophy and Religion* (London: Cambridge University Press).

DARWIN, Charles

2009   *The Origin of Species by Means of Natural Selection, or the Preservation of Favoured Races in the Struggle for Life* (Cambridge: Cambridge University Press).

DENNETT, Daniel C.

1995   *Darwin's Dangerous Idea: Evolution and the Meaning of Life* (London: Penguin Books).

2006   *Breaking the Spell: Religion as a Natural Phenomenon* (New York: Viking Penguin).

DŌGEN 道元

1975   *Shōbōgenzō* (The Eye and Treasury of the True Law), vol. 1, trans. by Kosen Nishiyama and John Stevens (Tokyo: Nakayama Shobō).

DREES, Willem B.

2010   *Religion and Science in Context: A Guide to the Debates* (London and New York: Routledge).

DUMOULIN, Heinrich

1985   「東西の対話を促す華厳経」[The *Avataṃsaka sūtra* as a stimulus to the East-West Dialogue], *Sophia* 34/2: 94–5.

2005   *Zen Buddhism: A History. Vol. 1: India and China* (World Wisdom).

ECKHART, Meister

2009   *The Complete Mystical Works of Meister Eckhart*, trans. and ed. by Maurice O'C Walshe (New York: Crossroad).

ENDŌ Shūsaku 遠藤周作

1969   *Silence*, trans. by William Johnston (Tokyo: Sophia University).

FRANK, Günter

2011   "Wie kam die Topik in die Theologie? Topik als Methode der Dogmatik bei Philipp Melanchthon und Melchior Cano," in Günter Frank and Stephan Meier-Oeser, eds., *Hermeneutik, Methodenlehre, Exegese* (Stuttgart: Frommann-Holzboog), 67–88.

2012   "Einleitung: Zum Philosophiebegriff Melanchthons," in G. Frank and F. Mundt, eds., *Der Philosoph Melanchthon* (Berlin: Walter De Gruyter, 2012), 1–10.

2017   *Topik als Methode der Dogmatik: Antike-Mittelalter-Frühe Neuzeit* (Berlin: Walter De Gruyter).

GADAMER, Hans-Georg

1973   *Wer bin Ich und wer bist Du? Ein Kommentar zu Paul Celans Gedichtfolge "Atemkristall"* (Berlin: Shurkamp Verlag).

1976   "Rhetorik und Hermeneutik," GGW 2: 276–91.

1977   "Klassische und philosophische Hermeneutik," GGW 2: 92–117.

1992 "The Expressive Power of Language: On the Function of Rhetoric for Knowledge," trans. by Bruce Krajewski, *Publications of the Modern Language Association of America* 107/2: 346–52.

2004 *Truth and Method*, trans. by Joel Weinsheimer and Donald G. Marshall (London: Bloomsbury).

GARDNER, Edmund G.

1898 *Dante's Ten Heavens: A Study of the Paradiso* (New York: Haskel House Publishers).

GEERTZ, Clifford

1973 *The Interpretation of Culture* (New York: Basic Books).

GEHLEN, Arnold

1988 *Man, His Nature and Place in the World*, trans. by Clare McMillan and Karl Pillemer (New York: Columbia University Press).

GOULD, Stephen Jay

1987 *Time's Arrow, Time's Cycle: Myth and Metaphor in the Discovery of Geological Time* (Cambridge, MA: Harvard University Press).

GRONDIN, Jean

2003 *The Philosophy of Gadamer*, trans. by Kathryn Plant (Acumen Publishing Limited).

GUTHRIE, Stewart

1980 "A Cognitive Theology of Religion," *Current Anthropology* 21/2: 181–203.

HABERMAS, Jürgen

2005 *Die Zukunft der menschlichen Natur: Auf dem Weg zu einer liberalen Ethik?* (Frankfurt a. M: Suhrkamp).

HARRISON, Edward

2000 *Cosmology: The Science of the Universe* (Cambridge: Cambridge University Press).

HASE Shōtō 長谷正當

1999 "Nihilism, Science, and Emptiness in Nishitani," *Buddhist-Christian Studies* 19: 139–54.

2009 "Nishitani's Philosophy of Emptiness in 'Emptiness and Immediacy,'" trans. by Robert F. Rhodes, *Japanese Religions* 34/1: 75–82.

HAYNES, Jeffrey

2009 "Introduction," in Jeffrey Haynes, ed., *Routledge Handbook of Religion and Politics* (New York: Rouledge), 1–7.

HAYES, Richard P.

1991 "Gotama Buddha and Religious Pluralism," *Journal of Religious Pluralism* 1: 65–96.

HEDGES, Paul

2017 "Multiple Religious Belonging after Religion: Theorising Strategic Religious Participation in a Shared Religious Landscape as a Chinese Model," *Open Theology* 3/1: 48–72.

HEGEL, G. W. F.

2003 *The Phenomenology of Mind*, trans by J. B.Baillie (New York: Dover Publications).

HEIDEGGER, Martin

1962 *Being and Time*, trans. by J. Macquarrie and E. Robinson (Oxford: Basil Blackwell).

1993 "What is Metaphysics?" in *Basic Writings*, ed. by David Krell (New York: Harper and Row), 93–110.

2002 *Grundbegriffe der Aristotelischen Philosophie, Gesamtausgabe, II Abteilung: Vorlesungen 1919–1944*, Band 18 (Frankfurt am Main: Vittorio Klostermann).

HEILER, Friedrich

1961 *Erscheinungsformen und Wesen der Religionen* (Kohlhammer).

HEIM, S. Mark

1995 *Salvation: Truth and Difference in Religion* (Maryknoll, NY: Orbis).

HEISIG, James W.

2001 *Philosophers of Nothingness: As Essay on the Kyōto School* (University of Hawai'i Press), 183–7.

2012 "The Misplaced Immediacy of Christian-Buddhist Dialogue," in Catherine Cornille and Stephanie Corigliano, eds., *Interreligious Dialogue and Cultural Change* (Eugene, OR: Wipf and Stock Publishers), 96–115.

HICK, John

1989 *An Interpretation of Religion: Human Responses to the Transcendent* (New Haven: Yale University Press),

1990 *Philosophy of Religion* (Englewood Cliffs: Prentice-Hall).

1995 *A Christian Theology of Religions: The Rainbow of Faith* (Louisville: Westminster/John Knox Press).

2006 *The New Frontier of Religion and Science: Religious Experience, Neuroscience, and the Transcendent* (New York: Palgrave Macmillan).

HIGASHI Senichirō 東 專一郎

1975 『同時性の問題』 [*The Problem of the Simultaneity*] (Tōkyo: Shōbunsha).

HONDA Masaaki 本多正昭

1973 「仏教的〈即〉の論理とキリスト教」 [The Buddhist logic of *soku* and Christianity] 『カトリック研究』 [*Catholic Studies*] 23: 1–25.

HUNTINGTON, Samuel P.

2004   *Who Are We? The Challenges to America's National Identity* (New York: Simon & Schuster).

IGGERS, Georg G.

1983   *The German Conception of History: The National Tradition of Historical Thought from Herder to the Present* (Middletown: Wesleyan University Press).

INGRAM, Paul O.

2008   *Buddhist-Christian Dialogue in an Age of Science* (New York: Rowman & Littlefield).

INWOOD, Michael

1999   *A Heidegger Dictionary* (Oxford: Blackwell).

JONAS, Hans

1994   *Das Prinzip Leben: Ansätze zu einer philosophischen Biologie* (Frankfurt am Main: Insel Verlag).

KALUPAHANA, David

1986   *Nāgārjuna: The Philosophy of the Middle Way* (Albany, NY: SUNY Press,).

KAMATA Shigeo 鎌田茂雄

1974   「法界縁起と存在論」[*Pratītyasamutpāda* in the *dharmadhātu* and ontology], in Mitsuyoshi Saigusa 三枝充悳, ed., 講座仏教思想 I: 存在論・時間論 (Tokyo: Risōsha), 95–136.

KASULIS, Thomas P.

2002   *Intimacy or Integrity: Philosophy and Cultural Difference* (Honolulu: University of Hawai'i Press).

KEEL Hee Sung

1996   "Jesus the Bodhisattva: Christology from a Buddhist Perspective," *Buddhist-Christian Studies* 16: 169–85.

KIM Seung Chul 金 承哲

1996   "Jesus the Bodhisattva: Jesus as Predicate," *Buddhist-Christian Studies* 16: 192–3.

1998   『해체적 글쓰기와 다원주의로 신학하기』[*Deconstructive Writing and a Theology of Pluralism*) (Seoul: Shigongsha).

2009   『神と遺伝子：遺伝工学の時代におけるキリスト教神学』[*God and Genes: Theology in an Age of Biotechnology*] (Tokyo: Kyōbunkan).

2012   『무주와 방황:기독교 신학의 불교적 상상력』[*Abiding and Erring: The Buddhist Imagination of Christian Theology*) (Seoul: Dongyon Publishing Co.).

KIMURA Kiyotaka 木村清孝
2004　「仏教と多元主義」[Buddhism and pluralism], in 『仏教と人間社会の研
究：朝枝善照博士還暦記念論文集』[*A Study of Buddhism and Human
Society: Papers in Honor of Dr. Asaeda Zenshō on his Sixtieh Birthday*]
(Kyoto: Nagata Bunshōdō), 517–28.

KLINGER, Elmar
1978　*Ekklesiologie der Neuzeit: Grundlegung bei Melchior Cano und Entwick-
lung bis zum Zweiten Vatikanischen Konzil* (Freiburg: Herder Verlag).

KNITTER, Paul
1985　*No Other Name? A Critical Survey of Christian Attitudes Toward the World
Religions* (Maryknolls: Orbis Books).
1996　"Cosmic Confidence or Preferential Option?" in Joseph Prabhu, ed., *The
Intercultural Challenge of Raimond Panikkar* (New York: Orbis Books),
177–91.
2009　*Without Buddha I could not be a Christian* (London: Oneworld Publications).

KUHN, Thomas
1962　*The Structure of Scientific Revolutions* (Chicago: University of Chicago
Press).

KÜNG, Hans
1993　"Kein Weltfriede ohne Religionsfride: Ein äkumenischer Weg zwischen
Wahrheitsfanatismus und Wahrheitsvergessenheit," in Hans Küng and
Karl-Josef Kuschel, eds., *Welrfrieden durch Religionsfrieden: Antworten aus
den Weltreligionen* (München: R. Piper,), 21–49.

LAWSON, E. Thomas
2000　"Towards a Cognitive Science of Religion," *Numen* 47/3: 338–49.

LE GOFF, Jacques
1988　*Medieval Civilization 400–500*, trans. by Julia Barrow (Hoboken: Blackwell Publishing).

LEFF, Michael C.
1983　"The Topics of Argumentative Invention in Latin Rhetorical Theory from
Cicero to Boethius," *Rhetorica: A Journal of the History of Rhetoric* 1/1:
23–44.

LEHMANN, Karl
1988　"Dogmengeschichte als Topologie des Glaubens: Programmskizze für
einen Neuansatz," in K. Lehmann, W. Löser, and M. Lutz-Bachmann, eds.,
*Dogmengeschichte und Katholische Theologie: Festschrift für Heinrich Bacht,
SJ, Alois Grillmeier, SJ, und Adolf Schönmetzer, SJ* (Würzburg: Echter Verlag), 513–28.

LEIDENHAG, Mikael and Joanna
2015 "Science and Spirit: A Critical Examination of Amos Yong's Pneumato-logical Theology of Emergence," *Open Theology* 1: 425–35.

LOHSE, Bernhard
1983 *Epochen der Dogmengeschichte* (Freiburg/Stuttgart: Kreuz Verlag).

LOVEJOY, Arthur
1960 *The Great Chain of Being: A Study of the History of an Idea* (New York: Harper & Brothers).

LÖWITH, Karl
1964 *From Hegel to Nietzsche: The Revolution in Nineteenth-Century Thought*, trans. by D. E. Green (New York: Columbia University Press).

LUEHRS, Robert B.
1975 "Christianity against Hisory: Franz Overbeck's Concept of the *finis chris-tianismi*," *Katallagete* 6: 15–20.

MASUZAWA Tomoko
2005 *The Invention of World Religions: Or, How the European Universalism was Preserved in the Language of Pluralism* (Chicago: University of Chicago Press).

MAYR, Ernst
1991 *One Long Argument: Charles Darwin and the Genesis of Modern Evolu-tionary Thought* (Cambridge: Harvard University Press).

MERLEAU-PONTY, Maurice
1964 *Sense and Non-Sense*, trans. by H. L. Dreyfus and P. Allen Dreyfus (Evan-ston: Northwestern University Press).

MOEVS, Christian
2005 *The Metaphysics of Dante's "Comedy"* (Oxford: Oxford University Press).

MONOD, Jacques
1971 *Chance and Necessity: An Essay on the Natural Philosophy of Modern Biol-ogy*, trans. by A. Wainhouse (New York: Alfred A. Knopf).

NIETZSCHE, Friedrich
1974 *The Gay Science* (New York: Vintage).

NIGG, Walter
2009 *Franz Overbeck: Versuch einer Würdigung* (Zürich: Römerhof).

NISHIDA Kitarō 西田幾多郎
2002 「永遠の今の自己限定」[The self-determination of the eternal now], in 『西田幾多郎全集』(Tokyo: Iwanami Shoten) 5: 143–82.

NISHITANI Keiji 西谷啓治
1940 『根源的主体性の哲学』[*A Philosophy of Elemental Subjectivity*], NKC 1.
1977 「ニヒリズム・宗教・科学」[Nihilism, religion, science], NKC 21: 5–14.

1982   *Religion and Nothingness*, trans. by Jan Van Bragt (Berkley: University of California Press).

1985   "An Interview with Keiji Nishitani," conducted by Ejiri Yoshiaki and Jeff Shore, FAS *Society Journal*, Summer: 3–9.

1986   "The Starting Point of My Philosophy," FAS *Society Journal*, Autumn: 24–9.

1990   *The Self-Overcomg of Nihilism*, trans. by Graham Parkes with Setzuko Aihara (New York: State University of New York Press).

2004   "Science and Zen," in F. Franck, ed., *The Buddha Eye : An Antology of the Kyoto School and Its Contemporaries* (Bloomington, IN: World Wisdom), 107–35.

NUSSBAUM, Martha C.

1990   *Love's Knowledge: Essays on Philosophy and Literature* (Oxford: Oxford University Press).

ODAGAKI Masaya 小田垣雅也

1983   『哲学的神学』[*Philosophical Theology*] (Tōkyō: Shōbunsha).

ODIN, Steve

1982   *Process Metaphysics and Hua-yen Buddhism: A Critical Study of Cumulative Penetration vs. Interpenetration* (Albany: SUNY Press).

ŌHASHI Ryōshuke 大橋良介, ed.,

2011   *Die Philosophie der Kyōto-Schule: Texte und Einführung* (Freiburg im Breisgau: Verlag Karl Alber).

OTT, Heinrich

1959   *Denken und Sein: Der Weg Martin Heideggers und der Weg der Theologie* (Zollikon: Evangelischer Verlag).

1967   *Dogmatik, Theologie VI x 12 Hauptbegriffe* (Freiburg/Stuttgart: Kreuz Verlag).

1968   "Das Hermeneutische als das Unumgängliche der Philosophie," in Heinz Robert Schlette, eds., *Die Zukunft der Philosophie* (Olten: Walter-Verlag), 87–104.

1981   "Zur Wirkungsgeschichte der Entmythologisierungs-Debatte," in Karl Jaspers and Rudolf Bultmann, *Die Frage der Entmythologisierung* (München: R. Piper & Co. Verlag), 7–26.

1988   "Geschichte und Eschatologie," in R. Brändle and E. W. Stegemann, eds., *Franz Overbecks unerledigte Anfragen an das Christentum* (Munich: Chr. Kaiser Verlag), 182–95.

OVERBECK, Franz

1995   *Werke und Nachlass*, ed. by Barbara von Reibnitz (Stuttgart: Metzler), 9 vols.

2005   *How Christian is our Present-Day Theology?*, trans. by Martin Henry (London: T & T Clark International).

PACI, Enzo

1998   *Phenomenological Diary*, trans. by Luigi M Bianchi. www.yorku.ca/lbianchi/paci/diary_ver_02.html

PANIKKAR, Raimon

1975   "Verstehen als Überzeugtsein," in Hans-Georg Gadamer and P. Vogler eds., *Neue Anthropologie*, vol. 7 (Stuttgart: Thieme), 132–67.

1979   *Myth, Faith and Hermeneutics: Cross Cultural Studies* (New York: Paulist Press).

1984   "Religious Pluralism: The Metaphysical Challenge," in Leroy S. Rouner, ed., *Religious Pluralism* (Notre Dame: University of Notre Dame Press), 97–115.

1987   "The Jordan, the Tiber, and the Ganges: Three Kairological Moments of Christic Self-Consciousness," in John Hick and Paul Knitter, eds., *The Myth of Christian Uniqueness: Toward a Pluralitic Theology of Religions* (Maryknoll, NK: Orbis Books), 89–116.

1993   *A Dwelling Place for Wisdom* (Louisville: Westminster/ John Knox Press).

1995   *Invisible Harmony: Eassays on Contemplation and Responsibility*, ed. by Harry James Cargas (Minneapolis: Augsburg Fortress Press).

1999   *The Intrareligious Dialogue* (Mahwah, NJ: Paulist Press).

2010   *The Rhythm of Being: The Unbroken Trinity* (Maryknoll, NK: Orbis Books).

PANNENBERG, Wolfhart

1961   (ed.), *Offenbarung als Geschichte* (Göttingen: Vandenhoeck & Ruprecht).

1979   "Erwägungen zu einer Theologie der Religionswissenschaft," in W. Pannenberg, *Grundfragen Systematischer Theologie: Gesammelte Aufsätze* (Göttingen: Vandenhoeck & Ruprecht), 252–95.

1985   *Anthropology in Theological Perspective*, trans. by M. J. O'Connell (London & New York: T & T Clark International).

PARKES, Graham

1990   "Introduction," NISHITANI 1990, xv–xxviii.

PENCE, Gregory E.

2002   *Brave New Bioethics* (Lanham: Rowman & Littlefield Publishers).

PETER, Niklaus

2000   "Ernst Troeltsch auf der Suche nach Franz Overbeck: Das Problem des Historismus in der Prespektive zweier Theologen," *Troeltsch-Studien* 11: 94–122.

PETERS, Ted

1997   "Cloning Shock: A Theological Reaction," in Ronald Cole-Turner, ed., *Human Cloning: Religious Responses* (Westminster John Knox Press) 12–24.

2018 "Science and Religion: Ten Models of War, Trust, and Partnership," *Theology and Science* 16/1: 11–53.

PHAN, Peter C.
2003 "Multiple Religious Belonging: Opportunities and Challenges for Theology and Church," *Theological Studies* 64: 495–519.

PÖGGELER, Otto
1983 *Der Denkweg Martin Heideggers* (Pfullingen: Günther Neske).

PREUS, Christian
2014 "Introduction" to Philip Melanchton, *Commonplaces: Loci communes 1521* (Concordia Publishing House), 1–18.

PYUN Sun Hwan 邊鮮煥
1996 「타종교와 신학」 [Other religions and theology], 『변선환전집』 [*Collected Works of Sun Hwan Pyun*] (Seoul: Korean Institute of Theology), 1: 169–210.

RACE, Alan
1983 *Christians and Religious Pluralism: Patterns in the Christian Theology of Religions* (London: SCM Press).

RAHNER, Karl
1983 "On the Relationship between Natural Science and Theology, in *Theological Investigations*, vol. 19 (London: Darton, Longman & Todd), 16–23.

RICHARDS, Earl Jeffrey
1983 *Modernism, Medievalism and Humanism: A Research Bibliography on the Reception of the Works of Ernst Robert Curtius* (Halle-Saale: Max Niemeyer Verlag).

RUSE, Michael and Edward O. WILSON,
1986 "Moral Philosophy as Applied Science," *Philosophy* 61/236: 173–92.

RUSSELL, Bertrand
1935 *Religion and Science* (London: Oxford University Press).

SAITŌ Naruya 斎藤成也 and SASAKI Shizuka 佐々木閑
2009 『生物学者と仏教学者七つの対論』 [*Seven Dialogues on Science between a Buddhologist and a Biologist*] (Tokyo: Wedge).

SCHELER, Max
1976 "Mensch und Geschichte," in *Gesammte Werke, Späte Schriften* (Bern: Francke Verlag), 9: 120–44.
2009 *The Human Place in the Cosmos*, trans. by Manfred S. Frings, (Evanston: Northwestern University Press).

SCHMIDT-LEUKEL, Perry
2005 *Gott ohne Grenzen: Eine christliche und pluralistische Theologie der Religionen* (Gütersloh: Gütersloher Verlagshaus, 2005).

SCHMIT, Carl

1932 *Der Begriff des Politischen* (München: Verlag von Duncker & Humbolt).

SCHOLZ, Gunter

2015 "Wilhelm Dilthey und die Entstehung der Hermeneutik," *Hermeneutik, Methodenlehre, Exegese*, 11: 471–94.

SHULTS, F. LeRon

2014 *Theology After the Birth of God: Atheist Conception in Cognition and Culture* (London: Palgrave Macmillan).

SCHÜTZ, Paul

1963 *Freiheit-Hoffnung-Prophetie: Von der Gegenwärtigkeit des Zukünftigen* (Hamburg: Furche Verlag).

SCWEITZER, Albert

1974 "Das Christentum und die Weltreligionen. Zwei Aufsätze zur Religionsphilosophie," *Gesammelte Werke* (Zurich: Buchclub Ex Libris), 2: 665–716.

SEKIDA Katsuki 関田一喜, trans.

1977 *Two Zen Classics: Mumonkan and Hekiganroku* (Tokyo: Weatherhill).

SLOTERDIJK, Peter

2005 *Regeln für den Menschenpark: Ein Antwortschreiben zu Heideggers Brief über den Humanismus* (Frankfurt a. M: Suhrkamp).

SMITH, Jonathan Z.

1998 "Religion, Religions, Religious," in Mark C. Taylor, ed., Critical Terms for Religious Studies (Chicago: University of Chicago Press), 269–84.

SOMMER, Andreas Urs

1997 *Der Geist der Historie und das Ende des Christentums. Zur "Waffengenossenschaft" von Friedrich Nietzsche und Franz Overbeck* (Berlin: Akadamie Verlag).

SUZUKI Daisetsu (Teitarō) 鈴木大拙 (貞太郎)

1961 *Essays in Zen Buddhism,* First Series (New York: Grove Press).

SUZUKI Kōh 鈴木 享

1983 『響存的世界』 [*A Resounding World*] (Tokyo: San-ichi Shobō).

TAKAKUSU Junjirō 高楠順次郎

1973 *The Essentials of Buddhist Philosophy*, ed. by Wing-Tsit Chan and Charles A. Moore (Westport: Greenwood Press).

TAKEDA Ryūsei 武田龍精

2008 「親鸞浄土教再解釈の一視座：宗教多元時代における浄土教の脱構築」 [A perspective for the reinterpreting Shinran's Pure Land teachings: The Deconstruction of Jōdo Buddhism in an age of religious pluralism], 『宗教研究』 [*Religious Studies*] 82/2: 497–522.

TAYLOR, Mark C.

   1984   *Erring: A Postmodern A/theology* (Chicago: University of Chicago Press).

THOMAS, Terence

   1995   "Convergence and Divergence in a Plural World," in F. J. Parrella, ed., *Paul Tillich's Theological Legacy: Spirit and Community* (Berlin: Walter de Gruyter), 18–42.

TILLICH, Paul

   1924   "Ernst Troeltsch: Versuch einer geistesgeschichtlichen Würdigung," *Kant-Studien* 29: 351–8.

   1964   *Christianity and the Encounter with the World's Religions* (New York: Columbia University Press).

   1967   "The Significance of the History of Religions for the Systematic Theologians," in Joseph M. Kitagawa, ed., *The History of Religions. Essays on the Problem of Understanding* (Chicago: University of Chicago Press), 241–55.

TROELTSCH, Ernst

   1913   "Über historische und dogmatische Methode in der Theologie," in E. Troeltsch, *Gesammete Schriften*, Band II (Tübingen: J. C. B. Mohr), 729–53; English translation by Jack Forstman, "On the Historical and Dogmatic Methods in Theology," {http://faculty.tcu.edu/grant/hhit/Troeltsch,%20On%20the%20Historical%20and%20Dogmatic%20Methods.pdf}.

   1922   *Der Historismus und seine Probleme*, erster Buch, *Das logische Problem der Geschichtsphilosophie: Gesammelte Schriften,* Band III (Tübingen: J. C. B. Mohr Verlag).

   1925   "Meine Bücher," in Hans Baron, ed., *Gesammelte Schriften,* Band IV, *Aufsätze zur Geistesgeschichte und Religionssoziologie* (Tübingen: J. C. B. Mohr Verlag), 3–18.

   1971   *The Absolutness of Christianity and the History of Religions*, trans. by David Reid (Richimond: John Knox Press).

   1980   "The Place of Christianity among the World Religions," in John Hick and Brian Hebblethwaite, eds., *Christianity and Other Religions: Selected Readings* (Glasgow: Collins), 11–31.

VAN BRAGT, Jan

   1982   "Translator's Introduction," NISHITANI 1982, xxiii–xlv.

   2003   "Multiple Religious Belonging of the Japanese People," in CORNILLE 2003, 7–19.

   2014   *Interreligious Affinities: Encounters with the Kyoto School and the Religions of Japan*, ed. by James W. Heisig and Kim Seung Chul (Nagoya: Nanzan Institute for Religion and Culture).

VATTIMO, Gianni

   1988   *The End of Modernity: Nihilism and Hermeneutics in Postmodern Culture*, trans. by Jon R. Snyder (Baltimore: The Johns Hopkins University Press).

VICO, Giambattista
   1948   *The New Science,* trans. by T. C. Bergin and M. H. Fisch (New York: Cornell University Press.

VON HÜGEL, Friedrich
   1924   "Einleitung," in Friedrich von Hügel, ed., *Der Historismus und seine Überwindung: Fünf Vorträge von Ernst Troeltsch* (Berlin: Pan Verlag Rolf Heise), v–xii.

VON BRÜCK, Michael and Whalen LAI
   1997   *Buddhismus und Christentum: Geschichte, Konfrontation, Dialog* (München: Verlag C. H. Beck).

VON WEIZSÄCKER, Carl Friedrich
   1949   *The History of Nature,* trans. by F. D. Wieck (Chicago: The University of Chicago Press).
   1991   *Der Mensch in seiner Geschichte* (München: Carl Hanser Verlag).

WERBICK, Jürgen
   2015   *Theologische Methodenlehre* (Freiburg: Herder Verlag).

WHITEHEAD, Alfred Nort
   1925   *Science and the Modern World* (New York: The Macmillan Company).

WILMUT, Ian, Keith CAMPBELL, and Colin TUDGE
   20002   *The Second Creation: Dolly and the Age of Biological Control* (Cambridge, MA: Harvard University Press).

WILSON, Edward O.
   1978   *On Human Nature* (Cambridge, MA: Harvard University Press).
   1998   *Consilience: The Unity of Knowledge* (New York: Alfred A. Knopf).

WOLFE, Judith
   2013   *Heidegger's Eschatology: Theological Horizons in Martin Heidegger's Early Work* (Oxford: Oxford University Press).

WOODBRIDGE, Frederick J. E.
   1981   "Pluralism," in James Hastings, ed., *Encyclopaedia of Religion and Ethics*(London: T & T Clark), 10: 66–70.

WUTHNOW, Robert
   1998   *After Heaven: Spirituality in America since the 1950s* (Berkley: The University of California Press).

YONG, Amos
   2012   *The Cosmic Breath: Spirit and Nature in the Christainity-Buddhism-Science Trialogue* (Leiden: Brill).
   2003   *Beyond the Impasse: Toward a Pneumatological Thelogy of Religions* (Eugene: Wipf and Stock).

Yosihara Eikaku 吉原瑩覚

1973 「世界と法界」 "The World *loka-dhātu* and the *dharma-dhātu*,"『神戸商船大学紀要 第1類 文科論集』*Review of Kobe University of Mercantile Marine,* Part 1: Studies in Humanities and Social Science 21: 1–16.

Yuasa Hiroshi 湯浅 弘

2004 「日本におけるニーチェ受容史瞥見：西谷啓治のニヒリズム論をめぐって」 [An Essay on Japanese Readings of Nietzsche: Keiji Nishitani's Theory of Nihilism] 『川村学園女子大学研究紀要』[*Journal of Kawamura Gakuen Woman's University*] 15/2: 97–111.

Žižek, Slavoy

2004 *Organs without Bodies: Deleuze and Consequences* (New York: Routledge).

General Index

Abe Masao 阿部正雄, 143

Abfall, 76

absolute, 39–40, 47, 116, 137, 143, 146; a. affirmation, 101; death-*sive*-life, 101; a. equality, 113; a. negation, 102, 109, 116, 143; a. negativity, 101; a. non-attachment, 110, 112–13, 117

absoluteness of Christianity, 40, 42–3, 46, 48–9, 73, 128

abyss, 75–6, 85–7, 99–100, 106–7, 110, 114–15, 117–18, 144; a/ of nihilism, 118; a. of nihility, 100, 107, 110, 114–15, 117–8

advaitic pluralism, 130–1, 146–7

aesthetics, aesthetic experience, 19, 41, 89

Age: of biological control, 82; of religious pluralism, 125; of science, 22–3; of the death of God, 155

agnosticism, 68

aktuell, 8–9, 15

All in One, 136, 145

Alsberg, Paul, 65

alterity, 124, 129

amor fati, 103, 115

anātman, 139

ancilla theologiae, 51, 56

Andere, der absolute, 51

animals, 30, 59, 61–3, 66–8, 103

annihilationism, 137

a. nothingness, 101, 108, 158; a. objective truth, 47; a. One, 33, 49, 118, 130, 143; a. truth, 14, 81, 148; a. unity, 143

anthropology, 38, 61–3, 66, 85

anxiety, 53, 61, 63, 76, 82, 126; a. of religious pluralism, 84

apologetics, 43, 80

Aristotle, 15, 19, 30, 88, 91, 149; *Rhetoric*, 19; *Topica*, 15

Asian: Christians, 56, 133, 136–8, 142; religions, 131, 133

assimilation theory of truth, 133

Assmann, Jan, 122–6, 159

asti, 135

astronomy, 22–3, 29

atheism, 31, 68, 98, 101, 108, 119, 158

Augustine, 132

autonomy, 119, 145

Avataṃsaka sūtra, 136, 139, 161

avidyā, 135

awakening, 37, 85–6, 89, 100, 102, 107–8, 118, 132, 134–6, 139–40, 143

Baldi, Pierre 59–61, 118, 153

Barbour, Ian, 22–3, 35, 150

Barrett, Justin, 70

Barth, Karl, 38, 77, 154–5

Beck, Ulrich, 125

Being, 19, 48, 65, 91, 110, 159; B.-towards-death, 77, 154; great chain of b., 30; transcendent B, 44; b.-*sive*-nothingness, 112

Being-there. See *Dasein*

Berger, Peter, 125, 152, 159

Bernhardt, Reinhold 152

Big Bang theory, 30, 35

Bindestrich-Ethik, 83

bioethics, 32, 83, 85

bioinformatics, 59

biology, biological, 13, 22, 28–32, 35, 59, 61–2, 68, 82; b. fact, 68; b. iconoclasm, 31; bio-psychic model, 64

biotechnology, 32, 81, 83, 155

Blue Cliff Record, 147